RACING AHEAD

RACING AHEAD

A COMPETITOR'S GUIDE
TO MOTORSPORT

GLYN THOMAS

MOTOR RACING PUBLICATIONS LTD
Unit 6, The Pilton Estate, 46 Pitlake, Croydon CR0 3RY,
England

First published 1995

British Library Cataloguing in Publication Data
Thomas, Glyn
    Racing Ahead:Competitor's Guide to
    Motorsport
    I. Title
    796.72

    ISBN 0-947981-89-6

Printed in Great Britain by
Hartnolls Limited, Bodmin, Cornwall

Contents

Why compete? Motorsport for all; Karting;
Sprinting; Hillclimbing; Drag racing; Autocross;
Autotests; Trials - Production car, Class reliability,
Sporting; Cross-country; Rallying; Rallycross;
Historic Rallying; Circuit Racing; Licences.

A professional approach; Help - the value of
friends; Mechanical expertise; Pit crew; Time
management; How to budget; Working facilities;
Tools; In the paddock; Transport - Advantages and
Disadvantages.

What car?; Buying secondhand - Authenticity,

"...You know your ladder from your snake,
You know the throttle from the brake,
You know a straight line from a curve,
You've got a lot of nerve..."

Peter Gabriel
From the song *Steam*

Introduction

The idea of writing this book first came to me during my second year of motor racing when I was struck by how little information was available to anyone contemplating entering motorsport, or who was already racing but wanted to improve. Looking around various bookshops, I found lots of coffee-table-type art books with some fantastic photos of Formula One cars, together with a plethora of biographies on Nigel Mansell, but with all due respect to him, nothing of any use to a club racer with grubby fingernails. I felt sufficiently offended to start writing, and I just kept on going.

Throughout, I have tried not to distinguish between amateur and professional racing because, as with so many sports, the terminology tends to give the impression that the amateur is somehow unprofessional, and therefore by implication less competent - which is plainly not the case. Countrywide, you will see many private competitors who race for fun and whose approach has been planned and executed with all the detailed excellence of an established race team. This book, of course, is not aimed at them, but rather at all the other racers who, perhaps, like me, would welcome any advice from a fellow-competitor which will enable them to get the job done just that little bit better and, because of that, even more enjoyably.

Although I set out with the intention of providing as much detail as possible, there are certain specialist and highly technical areas of motorsport, notably engine preparation and suspension development, that have already been covered expertly by authors with the necessary skills and experience of their particular subject, and therefore these do not form a part of this book.

Instead, I have emphasized preparedness in its broader context, along with procedures, right through from choosing the most appropriate branch of the sport and the car with which to compete in it, to obtaining the necessary licence, personal and car preparation, pre-race testing and then the race-day countdown from signing-on through to the event itself.

I have left to the end a chapter which I hope may well prove to be the most valuable of all: how to use sponsorship most effectively. Based on my own experience, it explains in some detail how not to go about it before setting out how to do the job properly.

Whilst the emphasis is firmly on circuit racing, for the benefit of newcomers I have taken the opportunity to identify the many alternative types of motorsport available for anyone contemplating active competition for the first time. There is, of course, a great deal that is common to all the disciplines, and so I hope and believe that much of what I have written in the context of circuit racing will prove equally useful and relevant to those who have chosen to enter the sport through a different branch.

Despite modest protestations, I must thank John Blunsden,

my publisher, for recognizing that this book has a niche, and for having the confidence to publish the words of someone whose status as an author is similar to the one he enjoys as a racer but who has endeavoured to pursue both activities with a certain amount of professionalism.

Finally, I must thank Keith Wisdom, Managing Director, of Harton Heating Appliances who has supported my racing campaign for the past three years. At the time of writing I am about to enter the Phoenix Petroleum Challenge in a MG Metro Turbo. (Please come over and speak – I won't bite!)

Racing certainly concentrates the mind, and it has brought me moments which have ranged in quick succession from near-hysteria to euphoria – like entering Paddock Hill Bend three-abreast on the first lap, to acknowledging the chequered flag with the car still intact. I hope the following pages will help you through the first situation and reward you with the second.

January 1995   GLYN THOMAS

Acknowledgements

Whilst researching this book I have had the good fortune to come into contact with many people whose business is motorsport and who have taken the time from their busy schedules to help me. Likewise, I am grateful for the encouragement and interest taken by friends and colleagues. In particular I wish to thank the following individuals and organizations:

BARC; BMSAD; *Cars and Car Conversions*; Steve Dale; Du Pont International; Dunlop; Mike Garton; Jaybrand Racewear; Alex Mosedale; Ben Parry; RACMSA; Jim Russell's British Academy of Motor Sport; Martin Short; Graham M Smith; Snell Memorial Foundation; Dunlop SP Tyres Ltd; Colin Valentine (BTRDA).

Front cover photograph by Steve Jones. All other photographs supplied by the author or MRP. Circuit graphics by InHouse Communications.

CHAPTER 1

An introduction to motorsport

"You may find this difficult to believe, but winning isn't as easy as it looks."
Ron Dennis
The Independent, July 9, 1988

Mention the magic words 'Motor Racing' and most non-aficionados will instinctively think of Formula One and the TV-hyped superstars like Nigel Mansell, Michael Schumacher, or whoever happens to be making the biggest headlines at the time. Certainly, Formula One, through the medium of that mesmerizing 'box' in front of which countless thousands drop off to sleep after a heavy Sunday lunch, reaches motor racing's biggest audience - even if you only count those who remain awake throughout the two hours during which the procession of earthbound missiles circulate in seemingly ever more predictable formation on just 16 weekends of the year.

But as many of us know, despite all the hype and the

ludicrously huge amounts of money poured into it, Formula One is but the tip of the motor racing iceberg, the real substance and broad base of which provides genuine enthusiasts with the opportunity not only to watch the action at the trackside at an affordable price but, if the desire is there, to actually become part of that action.

Almost every weekend of the year, competitors from all backgrounds assemble to race all sorts of cars in a wide variety of disciplines. These range from sprinting the family saloon around a cone-lined course set out on a local airfield, to the more competitive arena of racing purpose-built single-seaters at permanent race circuits. Most of the events are low-profile, and only very rarely are there any prizes beyond the odd cup and garland, yet this does not detract from the enjoyment whether you are in the driver's seat or spectating from the trackside. It is a sport that assails all the senses, from the smell of rubber, oil and petrol to the sound of engines in full song, and it has an immediacy that is missing from televised or stadium-based events. If you haven't already sampled it, my advice is to get out there and soak up the atmosphere, and don't be surprised if spectating leads to an uncontrollable eagerness to 'have a go'.

Why compete?

This may seem a rather odd question, but it is one that should be addressed seriously from the moment you first contemplate motorsport, and then answered with care because your motives will largely determine the type of racing that is most suited to you. If you simply want to get out at the weekend and have some fun, there are plenty of clubman events which can be entered in your own car, which is a particular advantage if you have a low budget and are still unsure as to the extent to which the sport will appeal to you as a leisure activity. At the other end of the scale, however, if you are thinking of pursuing a career as a driver, you will need to map out your progression with clinical precision and single-mindedness in order to achieve your aims, and the younger you can start the better; racing drivers, rather like policemen, seem to get younger each year.

As you become more involved in the sport, at whatever level, you will realize just how expensive an activity it can become, so it is essential to define your ambition early in order to to prevent any unnecessary waste of time and money. Because of its importance, this point will continue to be emphasized through the early chapters.

In many ways, choosing a race discipline that best suits you is rather like the dilemma you probably faced at school when, at a time when even your next summer holiday seemed like a decade away, you were asked by a careers teacher to make decisions that would shape your whole future. However, there are a few pointers to guide you in the right direction.

In the main, karts and single-seater cars are to be seen being driven to their limit by young hopefuls who nurse ambitions of future success in the more senior championships and are motivated by the ultimate dream of a drive in a Formula One car with its concomitant fame and fortune. Whilst some drivers might deny this to be the case, very few of them would ever turn such a chance down. The majority of the top F1 drivers have worked their way up from similar humble beginnings, and competitors in these formative junior formulae are certainly in a better position ultimately to succeed than those competing in other forms of motorsport such as, for example, rallying or hillclimbing.

If you seriously believe you are potentially an F1 World Champion then I applaud you for setting your sights so high. I also trust that you are not only young and naturally talented, but also very rich, as motorsport at its highest level is a marriage of driver and machine that requires a large -

and ongoing - dowry in order to succeed.

Dream by all means, though, as hopefully this will lead to you becoming involved in the sport, but as you will soon discover, most competitors are not the slightest bit interested - let alone eligible - to escalate to such heights. Some may argue that the expression "It's taking part that counts" is just an excuse used by losers and that winning is everything, but if this were the case why do so many people take part each weekend with no realistic chance of winning?

In reality, for the majority of drivers at club level the act of competing is itself the *raison d'être*, whether it is in a sprint on a cold, wet airfield or thundering through a forest stage. Naturally, everyone would like to win, but in most cases sufficient satisfaction is to be derived from improving their personal performance or their finishing position relative to their peers - and from the sheer thrill of the driving itself.

Motorsport for all
If you believe that motorsport is just for dashing young men, such a myth has been effectively challenged in recent years by the increase in the number of women drivers who have been participating at all levels, a trend that is not only overdue, but welcome.

Proof that gender is no disadvantage when competing is ably provided by the likes of Jinny Hyde, who was just pipped to first place in the 1993 Hot Hatchback series run by the 750 Motor Club, and Tina Cooper, who was unassailable in the Unipart DCM Mini Se7en Challenge that same year. No doubt it will take a little time, but I am sure there will be a gradual increase in the number of women competing at the higher levels of motorsport as there are no physiological reasons - only prejudice - to prevent such a development.

Since 1991 the RACMSA has assessed and granted competition licences to drivers with a variety of disabilities including paraplegia, arthritis, multiple sclerosis, motor neurone and Parkinson's disease as well as visual and hearing impairment. In all cases, judgment is made by RACMSA officials of each individual on evidence of their practical competence and ability in relation to the demands of each discipline.

Disabled drivers, however, in addition to their physiological limitations, must also – like the aforementioned women – be prepared to cope with a certain amount of ill-judged prejudice, but provided they show sufficient determination, the opportunities are there for them to compete. In 1991, David Butler, a triple amputee, was granted the first competition licence specifically for disabled people. Since then David has been a notable driver in the MGOC MGB/C/V8 Championship and in 1994 competed in the Network Q RAC rally.

The whole area of disabled competitors and, in particular, the facilities required by spectators who may be disabled, are issues close to my heart through my 'day job', and I hope that both will be addressed more thoughtfully by event organizers in the future. As I write, there are a few circuits, such as Silverstone, Pembrey and Thruxton, where time and trouble has been taken to consider the needs of disabled people in their redevelopment proposals and provide them with good viewing areas and toilet facilities. Hopefully, other venues will follow their good example.

A choice of disciplines
So, what are the formative disciplines? A brief description of each of the main forms of motorsport, together with the RACMSA official definition where applicable, should help to answer this question and hopefully whet your appetite to find out more.

Included with each description is an explanation of the current licencing regime for each discipline, but as with the relevant Technical Regulations these can be subject to change each year and so should be taken as indicative only. In all cases you are advised to cross-check with the appropriate representative body and to consult the current RACMSA *Blue Book*, which is the number-one reference source for all competition drivers in the UK.

Karting

To feel the exhilaration of speed and close competition there is little that can compare with karting, which for many people will be their first experience of motorsport. Although propelled at relatively modest top speeds by road standards, the light construction of the karts enables them to accelerate rapidly, which, combined with ultra-sensitive steering and closeness to the ground, means that the impression of speed is much greater and adds to the immediacy of close racing.

Over the past few years a number of small, mainly indoor, kart tracks have sprouted to satisfy both the public's growing interest and provide corporate entertainment. These operations tend to provide a 'leisure' as distinct from a 'sporting' facility, rather like roller-skating or the cinema, but nevertheless they do offer a taste of what competitive karting is all about and can be good fun, especially if a group of you take part. Some of the larger, more established circuits are licenced by the RACMSA to stage official championship races; these cater more for the dedicated kart racer and have allied spares and repair facilities on site. It is at venues such as these that you can experience karting as a recognized and formative branch of motorsport.

Karting in this context requires considerable dedication if you have any hope of being successful. Like many other keenly contested sports, it is essential to start at an early age, and children from as young as eight to 12 years old are permitted in the low-cost Cadet Class. Occasionally there are a few problems caused by youthful exuberance, but this is only to be expected from such an age group, and it is certainly less dangerous at such a level if the racing is on an approved circuit with experienced instructors. Quite often the bad behaviour is more prevalent off-track, when parents become a little over-zealous with the well-being and success of their prodigies, but this is no worse than that experienced in the cut-throat world of junior football or tennis.

Other restrictions reflect the emphasis on this being a sport for the young, with classes based on age and engine size in the junior formulae, before eventual graduation to Gearbox classes for drivers over 16 years of age in 125-250cc karts. Technical regulations are both extensive and specific in order to ensure commonality and dispel the various 'tweaks' that can have such a dramatic effect on performance due to the lightness of the karts and their tuning potential.

A glance through the results of disciplinary cases published in the quarterly editions of *RACMSA News* nearly always carries a number of reports detailing various transgressions of karting regulations, together with lurid tales of driver misconduct. Make no mistake about it, karting is taken very seriously indeed. Even in the relatively low-key classes, large sums of money can be spent keeping the front-runners in their privileged positions, as no matter how expensive they are, the most minor of modifications and improvements are good value if the opposition cannot afford them and have to make do without.

At the top end of the sport are the Superkarts, whose looks and performance make them a miniature equivalent of their Formula One counterparts, with a great emphasis on aerodynamics and engineering excellence. Here, you are left in no doubt as to the large budget required in order to remain competitive and perhaps are reminded of the reason why so many of the world's top racing drivers began their formative years in karting.

Clothing requirements are much the same as for other

disciplines, with the need for approved helmet, gloves, boots and overalls, except that the latter need to be waterproof instead of flame-resistant as the cockpits are very exposed to the elements.

Speed events

"...an event in which cars run individually, even though two or more individual runs may be taking place concurrently, over a course exceeding 200m in length and in which the relative performance of the competitors is assessed by timing them over a given distance and the winner, or most meritorious performer, is the competitor who covers the distance in the least time. The term 'Speed event' will include hillclimbs, sprints, slaloms, drag races, autocross and other similar events." (RACMSA)

Sprinting

It is wonderful that in an age of extensive regulations and technical sophistication it is still possible to turn up at a sprint event in a standard road car and compete. You may not necessarily win, but this should not detract from your enjoyment of a branch of motorsport in which, because there is no visible competition – car against car – the most important factor is the quality of your own performance. Because of the marked increase in the cost of circuit racing fees over the past few years, many cars and competitors have moved across into the world of sprinting, and its popularity increases each year.

Sprinting is one of the oldest forms of motorsport, having been established shortly after the first cars became widely available, no doubt initially to settle some form of wager between drivers as to performance or personal skill. Sprints are occasionally held at race circuits, but more commonly they take place at flat venues – remote airfields are ideal – where a short course will be defined by marker cones and tyres, usually to form a number of bends and a chicane linked by straights.

Most sprint events attract a large number and variety of cars, so in the majority of cases the entries are divided into classes, depending on car type and engine size. These can range from Standard Production classes, consisting of road-going saloons, to single-seaters in the Racing Car classes. However, there is no allowance for the age of the car and the progress of technology, so it is not uncommon, for example, to see an original Mini-Cooper in the same class as a Suzuki Swift, or a Rover SD1 battling it out with an Aston Martin DB5. Therefore it is worth studying the class regulations carefully before seriously considering entering.

Cars complete the course singly against the clock, their times being measured automatically between crossing light beams at the start and finish (although some under-resourced clubs still have to resort to using the traditional stopwatch). For this reason, a timing strut – painted matt black so as to be non-reflective – must be fitted to each car at a specified height to ensure that the beams are broken effectively.

A typical day's sprinting will begin early, probably around 8am, with signing-on for upwards of 120 competitors, followed by scrutineering and a familiarization walk around the course. It always strikes me how sprinting is so quintessentially 'English' in its approach, nowhere more evident than when you discover that the scrutineers actually come to you, rather than the other way round. Furthermore, because the whole pace of the event is so much slower than circuit racing, for example, the scrutineers invariably take a genuine interest in you and your car as well as being concerned with safety requirements.

After the entire entry has been given one or two practice runs, the times of which do not form part of the competition, the whole event comes to a halt for a lunch break. This is for the benefit not so much for the competitors as for the officials, who may well have had to stand since dawn, cold and windswept, with nothing but a flag for company.

Following lunch, competitors are allowed a further two timed runs, the faster one one of which will be used to determine the results. Occasionally, the times are made cumulative, but this, of course, disadvantages the driver who has had a bad first run and who consequently might just as well pack up and go home. Consequently, whenever this system is used a more measured style of driving tends to prevail.

As in all forms of motorsport, safety at sprint venues is paramount, but thankfully the various rules in place are appropriate for the level of risk involved, which in sprinting is slight. Currently, the driver only needs flame-resistant overalls and a crash helmet; for cars competing in the Production class and licenced for the road, neither electric cut-out switches nor rollcages are required, although they are recommended. Therefore, in many cases this means that you can simply drive to the event, apply your competition numbers, change over to more suitable wheels and tyres, and you are ready for action. For other non-roadgoing classes the regulations are a little more exacting and akin to those required for circuit racing.

For a novice, sprinting is an ideal way into motorsport due to its low cost – the entry fee is typically under £50 – and the friendliness of the competitors generally; there tends to be a marked absence of prima donnas in the paddock. Another advantage is the ability to double-enter the car with a friend or partner, hence potentially halving the capital outlay and running costs.

From a spectating viewpoint, the amount of enjoyment to be derived from watching less than a minute's worth of effort is at times hard to imagine, but it is a very different situation from the driver's seat as the mind starts to concentrate on how to shave increments of time from each section of the course. Over a leisurely *al fresco* lunch, if you ponder the advantage to be gained from changing quickly up to second gear at the startline so to avoid wheelspin, it can be taken as clear evidence you have been hooked and are already past the point of no return. Although sprinting is truly 'amateur', this does not mean that it is not taken very seriously indeed by some, who can even be seen altering their tyre pressures as the sun disappears behind a cloud.

If you compete in your everyday transport, your first season should be all about learning and the fun of taking part. Inevitably, though, you will want to go quicker, and a decision will need to be made as to whether to modify the car in order to be more competitive or even to have a car just for racing. In case you had not yet realized, be warned: all forms of motorsport are addictive.

If there is a downside to this relatively cheap form of motorsport it is that, as touched on earlier, it is increasing in popularity and entries for events can no longer be guaranteed. At the time of writing, however, the RACMSA have announced that further venues are to be licensed, so at least this trend is being recognized and action taken.

Hillclimbing
Despite being closely allied to sprinting – and in many respects it is essentially an 'inclined sprint' – hillclimbing has its own particular characteristics, many of which are derived from the increased possibility of coming to grief. Get a corner wrong sprinting at North Weald aerodrome and you may take a bit of paint off your bumper if you are careless enough to hit a traffic cone or a tyre, but at Baitings Dam, as you swing the car upwards through walls of York stone, mistakes are a little more costly and tend to focus the mind accordingly.

Contrary to some misconceptions, hillclimbs are nothing to

do with off-road events, but take place at registered venues, some being steeped in history, with cars driving on a smooth but usually challenging Tarmacadam surface. Aside from the background scenery, however, which tends to be rather more interesting than that for sprinting, the two sports share the same basic technical regulations and class structure, although this does not necessarily mean that cars are interchangeable as their suspensions need to be set up differently.

As one can imagine, over the years hillclimbers have sought out the most beneficial type of car for each class and, within the scope of the regulations, the modifications necessary to increase handling and performance. This has resulted in the construction of one-off specials and even limited-production cars being designed and built specifically for hillclimbing such as those by Pilbeam and Mallock.

Nevertheless, as in sprint events, it is still possible to enter a standard road car and enjoy competing, which is one of the underpinning philosophies of club motorsport. As a prerequisite is a hill of some sort, the East and South-East in particular are poorly served, but to many travel is all part of the enjoyment. If you require further information it is best to talk to some of the competitors at your nearest venue or contact a local club for details of their championship. However, in all cases it is best to check with the organizers before you visit any hillclimb or sprint as most are closed to the public.

Drag racing
With the ultimate cars reaching speeds in the region of 280 miles per hour and covering a quarter-mile in under 5 seconds, it is not difficult to understand why drag racing is so popular and continues to be a growing sport in Europe.

Originating in the USA in the Forties, when bored teenagers would race their cars down the main street or 'drag' using the traffic lights as start lights, it is estimated that the modern fire and smoke-belching descendants of those early dragsters now attract almost 10 million spectators per annum, so it is big business. Admittedly the climate is more favourable there, but Americans are also renowned for their love of spectacle and all that is larger than life, so this level of support should also be seen as a cultural phenomenon.

The sport is gradually spreading throughout Europe, however, and continues to increase in popularity each year through a growing public awareness, undoubtedly helped by the coverage in recent years on satellite and cable television. Venues for some of the lower classes can be relatively small and unsophisticated, with the strip marked out with cones on deserted airfields rather like sprinting, but at the top level there are a number of purpose-built strips that consolidate and expand their facilities each year. Santa Pod Raceway is probably the most famous, being the first to open in Europe over 25 years ago and the only one in the UK which is licenced to stage international events. Currently attracting crowds in excess of 120,000 a year, it continues to be the premier strip outside North America and is worth visiting for the spectacle of the events alone, even if the thought of competing does not appeal; night races especially are very dramatic.

There are basically two broad types of drag racing: Sportsman and Professional. The former caters for the novice driver and consists of various classes of ascending speed and cost, beginning with 'Run What You Brung', where members of the public without RACMSA licences can compete in their normal road cars, testing their reactions and their cars' performance on the same drag strip as their heroes.

The Professional classes, as the name suggests, contain the ultimate cars in Pro Modified, Top Alcohol/Top Fuel

Dragster and Funny Car classes, all of which require considerable sums of money to build, develop and run.

Autocross
"*A speed event on a closed circuit with a grass or unsealed surface.*" (RACMSA)

Autocross events are run on grass-surfaced circuits which are small – straights are not permitted to be longer than 200m so as to limit speed – and mainly flat. Competitors compete against the clock, but subject to track size cars can be run simultaneously, and it is this racing element that adds to the immediacy of the event. The classes include a number for road/rally cars as well as specialist vehicles, and the technical regulations tend to follow those for circuit racing.

Autotests
"*...a competition in which marking during the event is based solely on a competitor's performance in manoeuvring tests. These tests may be at one or more sites on private property.*" (RACMSA)

Autotests are held in the main on Tarmacadam surfaces, the object being to complete a marked course in the quickest possible time. Known in the past as driving tests, Autotests examine the manoeuvrability of the car and the skill and ability of the driver in negotiating – both forwards and in reverse – what is often a tight and demanding series of tight bends and narrow gaps. Cars compete singly and are usually in standard form, although 'specials' with a tight turning circle, better all-round vision and modified brakes are also allowed (and usually win).

Trials
The *RAC Blue Book* includes regulations to cover three types of trial: Production; Classic Reliability and Sporting, each being different but linked by a common nomenclature.

Production car trials (PCTs)

"...a 'Trial' confined to vehicles of a production type over a course that is suitable to test equally the capabilities of cars of all sizes." (RACMSA)

This is the less specialized, and hence most popular, branch of trialling, the cars having to negotiate off-road terrain, both flat and inclined, through a series of marker poles without stopping. As the events are open to standard road cars, the course is relatively smooth, but being primarily grass and mud-surfaced it still requires skill and sensitivity at the controls to keep the car moving and in the right direction. The course is made up of 10 different sections or hills, each marked separately, and drivers incur penalties for hitting any of the markers or for stopping at any point, in which event the penalty incurred relates to the distance remaining to the end. Usually, competitors are given two attempts at the course in the morning, followed by a break for lunch, then further attempts during the afternoon, when the running order of the classes is reversed.

Basically, there are five different classes, ranging from front and rear-wheel-drive standard road cars exceeding 166in long, right through to 'specials' built specifically for the task, so there should be one that will suit you (although there is no class for 4WD cars because of their obvious advantages). As in all of the disciplines described so far, however, competing is one aspect, but winning is an entirely different proposition. With the class system favouring particular models, 'tweaks' such as varying individual tyre pressures and the judicious addition of ballast – such as lead cast into the bumpers – to enhance adhesion, are closely guarded by the elite. That said, as with all true amateur club events, the atmosphere is good, the competitors are friendly and the weather can usually be relied upon to be bracing.

Events are also inexpensive, usually costing between £10 and £15 with just the added cost of a gallon of petrol, and it can actually be a true family day out as passengers, whether adults or children, are allowed in the car when competing. As double entries are allowed, it is also possible to compare your driving abilities with your partner's.

A wide range of meetings are held nationwide, from those organized by local clubs to national events, with regional championships covering most areas. To prove that it truly is a low-cost form of motorsport, the 1993 BTRDA Championship was won by a Peugeot 205XS, with a MkI Golf GTI placed second, and both cars were driven to the events and used daily.

Classic reliability trials

"...a competition based on the ability to climb hills or traverse difficult sections non-stop and which may use the Public Highway for all or part of its route or may be entirely on private ground." (RACMSA)

Unlike PCTs, classic reliability trials cover large distances rather than keeping to a small defined course and tend to be based at venues established when the sport of trialling began (the first classic trial was the London-Lands End-London staged in 1908). The types of cars entered are fairly extensive, but tend to be of a historic nature to reflect the sport's heritage. Approximately 40 classic trials are organized each year, the most notable being the Edinburgh and Lands End events. At the Blue Hills Mine section of the latter I once spent a cold, wet day watching, amongst others, a local farmer in a tweed jacket – accompanied by his kids – coaxing a VW Beetle up a 40-degree shale incline, and I can thoroughly recommend the spectacle.

Sporting trials

"...a trial in which the marking during the event is mainly based upon the ability to climb hills or traverse difficult sections and in which the distance on a highway does not

exceed 50 miles." (RACMSA)

These events are rather like an off-road hillclimb featuring completely wild off-road tracks and all manner of rough terrain. This in turn has led to small purpose-built cars with such names as Kincraft and Facksimilie, stripped to basics and equipped with 'fiddle brakes' to become specialized climbing machines. There are approximately 90 sporting trials held each year.

Cross-country
The growth of off-road vehicles in Britain in recent years has led to a similarly marked increase in the number of motorsport events to cater for such vehicles in the form of trials, competitive safaris and orienteering events.

As the cars are already built to a very robust standard, only minimal modifications are needed to make the average 4WD car ready for competition. Events are increasing in number each year and are relatively good value for money when one considers the 'fun factor'.

Rallying
For some, rallying *is* motorsport, a fact borne out by the large number of participants at club level and the diehard enthusiastic spectators who flock to some of the major national stage events.

Rallying can broadly be divided into two categories: road rallying and stage rallying. Road rallies, as the name suggests, are held on public roads and can include a variety of different events ranging from economy runs and treasure hunts through to 12-car rallies, where the emphasis is placed on navigational skill and consistency rather than flat-out speed, for obvious reasons. Nevertheless, despite the allusion to these being low-key events they are still fiercely contested and highly enjoyable.

Stage rallies, on the other hand, in the main are held off-road and due to difficult and often dangerous terrain demand far more from the car in terms of preparation, and place a greater emphasis on the skill and experience of the driver. Special stages are timed sections on forest roads, tracks and disused airfields, covered with mud, loose shale dust or snow and ice, depending on the weather. Although far more expensive than road rallies, they nevertheless can still be relatively cheap at the outset – although this can swiftly change! – and at least involve instant participation, even if the car is virtually standard. This, and the fact that the events are a team effort of driver, navigator and support crew, make it an attractive discipline for the novice, who can usually edge his way into it after having helped or watched before taking the plunge.

Historic rallying
In recent years, a seemingly obsessional preoccupation with nostalgia has even touched the world of motorsport, with a growing participation and spectator interest in Historic rallying to the extent that it is now recognized as a particular discipline in its own right. After originating in the mid-Eighties, the sport has evolved quite rapidly, yet aside from the major events, which tend to attract serious entries driven by past masters coaxed out of retirement, it still remains largely the domain of the dedicated amateur, and now has a calendar of over 50 events nationwide, which include a good mix of stage and road rallies.

There are two main classes, divided according to the year of manufacture of the car: pre-1966 and 1966-1974 – although the latter class entries do not qualify for overall positions in the event due to the advantage of their age and associated advances in technology.

The wide variety of events open to Historic cars tend to mirror those open to their modern counterparts. At the top end of the sport there are Historic stage rallies, which can be quite demanding as they largely follow the same format as modern rallying events – the current Rally Britannia, which precedes the main Network Q RAC Rally, being the pinnacle event in Britain – whilst at a more modest level there are also a variety of mixed Autotest, navigational and regularity events that cater for everyone's interest and budget.

As one can imagine, due to the wide class system the types of cars eligible are numerous, ranging from big Austin-Healeys and Jaguar E-Types down to the more humble Austin A40s and Ford Zephyrs. Each of these cars has its place in the sport and the support of devoted spectators, who through them are perhaps reliving their youth. The age requirements for the vehicle do not preclude the fitment and use of modern safety devices such as rollcages and extinguishers, but in all other respects parts must be as originally fitted, including tyres, air filters and even specialist items such as sumpguards. Apart from the close examination of an eligibility scrutineer, some competitors also take a great interest in their rivals to check that their car is a true representation of the period. Therefore, it is necessary to undertake a lot of research before buying a suitable car and, once bought, care must be taken to ensure that any modifications are contemporary.

So, before you rush out and dust off the Austin 1800 that has been sitting forlornly in your garage for the past few decades, it is advisable first to contact the Historic Rally Car Register for some detailed advice on how to obtain a valid FIA logbook for the vehicle and other key information on getting started.

Rallycross
"...a timed event with several cars starting simultaneously which takes place on a closed circuit with a combination of sealed and unsealed surfaces." (RACMSA)

Rallycross originated in 1967 as a combination of rallying and circuit racing, the events being held at closed venues on a mixed surface of Tarmacadam and loose terrain, which invariably leads to thrills and often spills, especially in the wet. As the events consist of repetitive laps, this does away with the navigational demands of conventional rallying, and allows drivers and spectators alike a clear visual indication of relative positions.

Growing in popularity due to its relatively cheap entry costs and less risk of damage compared with stage rallying, the sport has attracted drivers both from that area of motorsport and from short circuit racing, especially since the technical regulations and class structure have been overhauled and simplified as follows:

Supercars – consisting of four-wheel-drive cars, except those in the Production class, with minimum weight limits depending on engine size.

Production – includes all Group N cars (including 4WD) complying with specific International Technical Regulations for Rallycross (this is for cars that can compete virtually as standard, aside from mild tuning and safety modifications).

Modified – caters for cars over 1,600cc that are not in either of the classes above, that is to say cars without 4WD, turbocharging or supercharging. Additionally, there are minimum weight limits for cars that are fuel-injected engines or mid/rear-mounted engines exceeding 2,850cc.

Modified 1600 – as its name suggests, this is similar to the modified class, but is restricted to cars with an engine size of less than 1,600cc.

A typical day's rallycross, like circuit racing, will begin with practice sessions for all drivers, but will then take a quite different approach by staging three sets of qualifying heats for each of the respective races. The heats determine the entry and start positions for the semi-finals by the fastest time set – a system which works fairly for 'fast but last' drivers, especially in respect of the last event of the day, which determines the overall event winner.

From a spectating viewpoint, you can get close to the action and actually see most of it as well, especially at the natural amphitheatre circuits such as Brands Hatch and Lydden Hill in Kent. Another advantage is that unlike rallying you do not need to traverse inhospitable flora in often appalling weather to do so – or perhaps I am just getting old! An additional major attraction is being able to see the true supercars such as the Metro 6R4, long banished from international rallying, in action on the same billing as standard cars to which the public can more readily relate. It is this last factor, combined with the recent rationalization of the class structure, that has led to growing support from motor manufacturers.

Circuit racing

"...a competition where two or more cars are started simultaneously from the same starting line and over the same course, and in which the winner is the competitor who first completes a specified distance including any handicap credit, or who completes the greatest distance in a specified time..." (RACMSA)

Circuit racing is the discipline which immediately springs to mind whenever people mention motor racing, and its popularity amongst spectators and drivers alike is assured by the adrenalin created by this uniquely close and competitive branch of motorsport.

With so many different types of cars being raced and with a disparate range of championships – and classes within them – covering everything from the humble Citroen 2CV to the full-blown fire-spitting touring cars and, amongst the single-seaters, the novice formulae right through to Formula One, there is in every sense, something for everyone.

Surprisingly, it is only since 1992 that any form of training and accreditation has been a requirement prior to a licence being granted for circuit racing. Until then a complete novice could be let loose on a track in a racecar without any test of competence, potentially to the detriment of themselves, fellow competitors and spectators. The RACMSA's move towards a test of proficiency, consisting of a practical and theoretical examination following a day's tuition at a circuit driving school, was therefore long overdue.

If you are applying for the first time or have allowed your licence to lapse for more than three years, you must first send the RACMSA a cheque (at the time of writing it was for £35), for which you will receive a 'Go racing' pack. This consists of an instructional video; a copy of the *RAC Blue Book*; details of the various circuits that run an approved Association of Racing Drivers course and, finally, an application form for your licence. On this must be written details of your medical condition, which means that you will require a medical examination by your local doctor, at a cost of about £40.

As can be seen, costs are already beginning to mount up. Yet if you are a complete novice you probably do not even know if you will like motor racing, let alone pass the necessary tests to allow you to participate. Therefore, to avoid making an expensive mistake, it may be advisable to book a trial course at your nearest circuit, even for just a few hours' tuition, just to check that the idea of going racing appeals as much as you thought it would.

The accredited course at a recognized Association of Racing Drivers School (ARDS) is mandatory, and although cynics may argue that this is an artificially created market of great benefit to race circuits, it still represents good value at around £120 when you consider that a typical race entry fee is not much less. The day's course will first involve a classroom briefing on safety and basic race techniques, such as how to set the car up properly for corners, and how to brake and overtake, followed in the afternoon by the opportunity to put this theory to practical use. You will be driven for a number of laps by an instructor, then you will exchange seats and be allowed to drive under tuition. Eventually, after a short break to collect your thoughts, you then drive for a few more laps to prove to the examiner that you are competent on the track. This forms the practical part of the test, which contributes half of the marks available. If this is completed satisfactorily it is back to the briefing room for a written paper based on the information that you should have absorbed during the day from the video, briefing session and driving on the track.

If you have acted properly and confidently on the track and achieved at least 60 per cent in the written paper, you are considered a 'Pass' and your application will be forwarded to the RACMSA with the recommendation that they issue a licence.

Licences
The licencing regime has changed considerably over the past few years, but hopefully it has now stabilized, and the accompanying chart indicates the main criteria at time of writing. The system is considerably simpler now, and for most low-key club events such as autotests and road rallies, you will need nothing more than a valid membership card for the organizing club. For events that demand a little more discipline and organizational constraints, however, it is necessary to hold a competition licence, although from the chart you will notice that apart from circuit racing none of the individual disciplines require any form of proficiency test. In most cases, therefore, it is simply a matter of completing the necessary forms and sending them off with a cheque, although you should also check the need for a medical examination. This is currently required for

competitors applying for race, truck and kart licences and is valid for a maximum of 24 months (12 months for competitors over 40 years of age).

Motorsport contains a rich and varied number of events and there should be at least one that will suit your particular situation, aspirations and budget. By talking to competitors and officials, plus careful observation, you should be able to obtain a rough idea of the costs, frequency, location and general feel of an event which appeals to you: are the competitors and officials friendly? Are the events popular or oversubscribed? Are they held at locations close to home or will it be necessary to travel extensively? Perhaps even more important is to check that there is indeed a future for the series you are contemplating; many championships have dissolved once manufacturer support has moved been on to newer models in their range.

Then, if you are still interested, it is worth getting in touch with the organizing club/body, either for the championship or general type of event, and request further details and regulations. Read these carefully as they will define eligibility to the last detail and hence the modifications which are permissible or illegal. It could then be beneficial to make contact with the club secretary, who may put you in touch with the technical scrutineer for the series in order to answer specific queries. Afterwards, why not talk to one of the companies that has already prepared a car or an engine for the race series, to get an idea of costs? Do not expect a plethora of race-winning tweaks from the latter, but at least they should be able to provide some guidance and may even be able to undertake some of the more specialist work for you.

Eventually, after attending a number of different events, you should be in a better position to assess which one appeals and then begin the next step of choosing a suitable car in which to compete. This, however, as we shall see, may be not quite as straightforward a task as one might expect, for several other issues now come into play, such as your location, your budget, and even the time of year. For example, if the season has just ended there will probably be plenty of secondhand cars on the market, but if it is already late autumn it may be too late to get a car ready for next year. Motorsport, in case you hadn't noticed, is all about timing.....

PIT
PASS
For conditions of admission see over
PEMBREY
3rd MAY 1993

Motor Racing is Dangerous
Your attention is drawn to the
warning printed on the reverse

CHAPTER 2

First-season essentials

"A racing driver is an artist, and driving is an expression of myself. It's not a job, but a definition of who I am.
John Watson
Sunday Times, August 2, 1981

Introduction

There will be times during your first season of competition when you will curse the day you ever decided to go motor racing, and perhaps others when you will wonder why you never took it up earlier, perhaps even as a career. However, in order to keep everything in perspective, it is as well to remember right from the start that there can only ever be one winner, and for the rest of the field, the best performance will in fact be only second-best, while for some unfortunates the dreaded letters 'DNF' (signifying Did Not Finish) may well appear alongside their name on the results sheet as a reminder of a day when all went far from well. Optimism is a positive ingredient in anyone's make-up, but it needs to be kept in proportion, and for your mental well-being it is probably wise to assume that during your first season you are likely to experience more moments of abject despair than of jubilation.

As an absolute beginner you will be faced with a very steep learning curve in a sport that is wholly unforgiving to the inexperienced, and where any errors of judgment will be accompanied by a cost in either time or money – but usually both. If you were concerned simply with the logistics of preparing the car, getting it to the circuit and then racing it, life would be relatively simple, but unfortunately, these are only the obvious aspects of going motor racing.

In addition, you need to be prepared for both the expected and the possible, which involve two subtly different levels of thought. For example, you may *expect* to have to check your tyre pressures, but it is *possible* that you will forget to pack the foot-pump. Similarly, you might *expect* to have to refuel the car after the practice session, but it is *possible* that there will be no pump fuel sold at the circuit. The sheer amount of information that you are expected to absorb means that at times all the odds will seem to be stacked against you. However, learning from others' mistakes is a cheap and preferable way of evening the odds.

With these sobering thoughts in mind, this chapter is intended to provide the uninitiated with some practical advice that will be useful early on as well as of continuing benefit as you progress. Some of it has been gained from personal experience, but the majority has been given to me by – or stolen from – fellow competitors, including commonsense issues that tend to get taken for granted when they occur, but are rarely passed on to the next person.

If one message is to emerge from your first season in motorsport, it is that you need to be organized. This applies even if you only want to enter low-budget clubman events.

Help – the value of friends

Motor racing may be one of the most exhilarating activities that you can enjoy on your own, but it can also be one of the most frustrating and tiring if you are faced with the task of having to do absolutely everything yourself. If you consider the total amount of time and effort involved in the activity, you will discover that an enormously disproportionate amount of it is invested in preparation compared with the actual race itself, which in most cases will probably last less than 20 minutes. It is not just the time and effort needed physically to prepare the car, but the fact that it seems to take over every spare moment you have, whether for planning, collecting parts, sewing name patches on your race suit (OK – having them sewn on, if you're lucky) and even getting to and from the circuit. Unless you really enjoy these peripheral aspects you are likely to become unhappy, and even if you do, tackling them all on your own is a bit much. Basically, you are going to need help.

The view that motor racing is a romantic, lonely activity is therefore a fallacy, just as it is to imagine that, on a Saturday afternoon, football fans visit grounds just to watch their team play for 90 minutes. An integral part of their enjoyment is the atmosphere of the event, from the tension and build-up on the way to the stadium, through the act of participation – if only by means of chanting from the terraces – and finally to the inevitable post-match discussions and arguments.

So, back on the grid, whereas you are alone in the car when the lights flash from red to green, much of your enjoyment will be derived from sharing the whole activity with friends and family. They in return will have valuable roles to play, ranging from holding spanners to restraining you when you want to set fire to the car when it all goes wrong. Only the sport of parachuting comes close to beating the number of bar-room tales that can be squeezed from motor racing; embroidery of the facts is also a common denominator.

This is an appropriate time to dwell briefly on the subject of personal relationships. From experience, this is an area conveniently glossed over in almost all books about sport, but it is an important one that should be considered at an early stage, before you become completely absorbed. As you will discover, motor racing is addictive, and it is very easy to become so involved in it that other seemingly less important issues will be swept aside and forgotten. This is fine if you are young, single and free, but look around the paddock at a typical club meeting and you will see that the majority of drivers are probably over 25, with a fair chance of them being attached. If you have a partner, therefore, be completely honest and declare upfront just how much time your racing is likely to consume – from my own experience this is usually three times as much as you had originally planned and anticipated. How you justify this dedication and sheer volume of time and effort is up to you because marriage guidance is a different – albeit closely associated – field of expertise. The ideal situation would appear to be where your new-found pursuit is shared and your partner plays an active role in it, perhaps even having a go themselves.

Help is likely to appear in many guises and should never be refused lightly, whether it be for stripping out the carpets, installing the rollcage or even – dare I say it – making the tea, although of course the presence of someone with mechanical expertise can be even more useful. Aside from the obvious benefits of assistance and camaraderie, it is also preferable from a safety aspect that you do not work alone, when it can be all too easy to work for too long without a break and in consequence lose concentration. Besides, there are some jobs involving heavy lifting or welding where help is essential.

Mechanical expertise

If you are not mechanically-minded you will need either friends who are or a bottomless bank account. Even if you are fortunate to have the latter you will still struggle to a degree because although money can pay for the car to be immaculately prepared, you will still need practical expertise both at the race track and during the time between events. It may seem obvious, but a car dedicated to racing is a breed apart from a road car, and its increased power and strength belie the fragile line between reliability and failure. It needs constant attention and maintenance because each time you race it you are pushing many of its components to their limit. If preventive maintenance is ignored, increased wear or lack of lubrication could mean a premature failure of a vital component. Some such failures may cause nothing more serious than a reduction in efficiency and a power loss through additional friction, but others could have more serious, even life or limb-threatening consequences: the unpredictability of which part may break, and when, can only be reduced by keeping the car in perfect shape.

Maintaining a car's optimum performance level is, of course, a vital ingredient of success, but setting up the car at testing sessions will require a clear understanding of suspensions, tyre technology and engine tuning. At the circuit a similar level of mechanical expertise will be required for the instant diagnosis of problems and their immediate solution, plus the chance of running repairs being required between practice and the race.

Squeezing every last bit of power without detriment to the car's handling or reliability demands a level of mechanical and engineering skill that cannot be picked up in a few minutes from reading a car manual, even if such a book existed, and I have to assume that either you or your support team have a detailed knowledge of at least the mechanical basics.

Pit crew

Aside from the obvious mechanical and other pre-race preparation tasks, members of a pit crew are required to perform other key functions that the driver either cannot or need not necessarily tackle personally. I differentiate between the two because the latter situation is a voluntary one: tasks can be removed from the driver to lessen his concerns about peripheral matters and so enable him to concentrate on the main function of preparing to race. The danger of this, of course, which is seen at its most extreme form when the Formula One stars arrive at the circuit by helicopter long after their support troops have been hard at work, is that the driver becomes remote from what is going on. Therefore, I am not suggesting that you, the driver, should become a *prima donna*, but rather that certain jobs are better carried out by someone else, such as checking on the best lap times being set in other race practice sessions, for example.

Of the tasks in the other category, which cannot be carried out by the driver because he is in the car, timekeeping and pit signalling are the most obvious and probably the most important. During practice the time of each lap must be recorded and reported to the driver on the following lap, using a pit board. Quite professional-looking boards are available fairly cheaply, so it is best to buy one of these rather than use something like a child's blackboard as I witnessed at one event – apparently the abacus was used for keeping a check on the number of laps left....

Assuming that there is no radio intercom system between the pits and the driver, the timekeeper must provide that vital link during the practice periods and the race, and be able to give important messages to the driver on the track. With all of your concentration focused on driving to the best of your ability, perhaps racing door-to-door with another car, this information, available for a split second as you pass the pits, must be clear and concise.

The information you will need during practice will include:
• Your time for the previous full lap (remember that this will refer to the lap before the one you are currently completing!).
• Alternatively, a +/- difference between a pre-arranged time. You may have raced on the circuit before and be able to use your previous fastest lap time as a benchmark.
• The estimated number of laps/time remaining in the session.

In the race, however, your lap time is largely irrelevant as it is your position and the relative speed of other cars that is important, unless of course there are additional points for setting the fastest lap.

Therefore, the information you will need in a race is:
• Your position in class or overall in the race.
• The time in seconds between you and the car ahead of you, or
• The time in seconds between you and the car following you.
• The number of laps completed.
• Also, if you are taking part in a long race requiring tyre/fuel stops, or it is a two-driver event, your pit crew will need to signal you to come into the pits at the relevant time.

Time management

If you have a full-time occupation, a family, and perhaps still cherish the odd hobby, you may be in for a shock. During your first season not only will you have to set aside the quite lengthy amount of time that the sport normally demands, but you will need to take into account the additional time needed to prepare the car because inevitably your lack of familiarity with it will slow you down.

One of the first problems you will encounter is knowing where to start. Faced with the need to do many different tasks, such as apply for your licence, work on the car, register for a championship and so forth, it can all be rather overwhelming, and at times it will seem as if your life is being completely taken over. Therefore, you must try to introduce a methodical approach which will help to define your objectives and prioritize them. You can try to do everything at once, but I have found to my cost that this only results in 'firefighting' each problem as it arises. This in turn leads to a lack of concentration and can cause the omission of an important task, ranging from the inconvenience of forgetting to pack your lunch to the more disruptive implications of putting-off applying for your racing licence until February. So, take some time to work out calmly what you need to do and write it all down. Once you have made a list, sort out the items into those that are dependent on other actions being carried out first.

Call it a checklist or a workplan, but what you will now have is a co-ordinated framework around which you can plan your activities in advance and allocate your most valuable resource – time. By assigning periods of time to each task and matching these to actual dates you will be able to know whether you are on schedule. A diary can be used to record all of this information, but a better option is to use a wallchart or year planner. This will enable you to see all of your racing commitments at a glance and even those domestic inconveniences such as dental appointments and scheduled visits by relatives. Once you have tried this you will wonder how you ever managed without it.

Another invaluable aid, which as usual I discovered far too late, is a notebook in which to write down everything important that otherwise might be forgotten. This can include telephone numbers of your local parts and racing accessories shops, the club secretary, circuits and so forth, as well as important information on the car such as valve clearances, when the oil was last changed, the tyre pressures and the suspension set-ups you established for each circuit. The list is endless.

The proper investment of time spent on careful advance planning will reap its reward later when you start to work on the car and eventually to race it. A word of warning, though: do not be surprised if you experience a strange phenomenon whereby the length of time left until your first race, once able to be measured in weeks, suddenly becomes definable on a wristwatch. Suddenly you will realize that the tasks that could have been completed months ago still remain to be done and begin to merge with new ones relevant to the coming weekend.

Whilst I am not advocating that you become obsessed with time and introduce a regime of military precision, the fact remains that planning, setting yourself reasonable deadlines and adhering to them will make your racing more professional, reduce risks and hopefully contribute to ultimate success. The key is to be in control off as well as on the track.

As an example of how to go about it the wrong way, let me recall a short story from my own catalogue of bitter experiences. At the end of one season I knew that the car would benefit from having negative camber arms fitted at the front and being lowered so as to reduce the centre of gravity. Within a few weeks this work had been carried out and I made a mental note to have the front wheel alignment checked as this might well have been disturbed. I knew it was a job that had to be done, yet I left it until gradually it became less important than getting the seat adjusted to the right position, finding the tent, and all the other jobs that demanded my time. As you have probably guessed, the task was forgotten and time rolled on.

At Cadwell Park, for the first race of the season, I joined the queue of other cars as we waited for our practice session. Half a lap after joining the circuit there was a clatter from the front of the car and a juddering through the steering wheel that felt as if I had puncture. Back in the paddock, however, we discovered that the driveshafts had been pulled out due to the wheels toeing-out too much. This had been caused by the combination of lowering the front of the car and fitting the new bottom arms accentuating the existing wheel alignment to a radical degree – just as I had thought might happen, all that time ago.

We worked frantically in an attempt to re-track the front wheels by dead reckoning, without the benefit of any gauges. A quick drive around the paddock road seemed to prove that the driveshafts were no longer about to pull out so I sprinted to see the Clerk of the Course. Hearing my plight, he kindly agreed to me completing a further single lap following the last practice session of the morning, which would enable me to qualify.

When you are having bad luck it tends to linger, and sure enough the last practice session was delayed and then it was ended with two separate accidents. As a consequence of this I was told to drive extremely slowly while the marshals cleared the track of broken cars and debris and therefore I was unable to get up to speed to establish how the *ad hoc* tracking adjustments had affected the handling of the car.

When my race was called to the assembly area I waited until last, knowing that I would be at the back of the grid with a 10-second penalty for practising out of session. As the grid completed the green flag lap everything seemed to be in order so I concentrated instead on the task ahead. When the lights changed to green I was held back for what seemed like an eternity, then the flag dropped and I raced to try to catch up with the rest of the cars that had disappeared into the distance. We later measured the tracking and found the wheels to be virtually parallel, which explained why the car was so sensitive that it followed every groove in the Tarmacadam – and why, at the top of the 'mountain' section, I lost control and pirouetted into the Armco barrier.

Money

All sorts of people will tell you that motor racing is a rich man's sport, and of course they are right. However, don't be put off – it need not be as expensive as you might think. Let us look at the basic amounts you will need in your first two years, excluding the actual cost of the car and any modifications necessary to make it comply with your class regulations or to be more competitive. For the purposes of this exercise it is assumed that you already have a suitable storage space, workshop facilities, tools and a friendly bank manager – if you have never met him, this will surely change.

Description	Year 1	Year 2
RACMSA 'Go racing' pack	35	-
Medical examination	40	-
ARDS examination	20	-
Licence fee (Nat B)	35	35
Safety clothing – overalls	200	-
undergarments	70	-
helmet	100	-
hand/footwear	100	-
Championship registration	30	30
Race fees - £90 per race x 10	900	900
Transport – 10 races average 150-mile round trip, 20mpg at £2.40 per gal	180	180
Maintenance – £25 per race average for parts, oil, filters, etc	250	250
Replacement set of tyres (multiply by 5 if running slicks)	160	160
	£2,120	£1,555

Of course, what this neat list omits are the less obvious costs that are more difficult to quantify. First, here are the additional items that will need to be paid for in real cash terms:
- A suitable towing vehicle – if available already, is it fitted with a tow bar?
- Trailer purchase/hire.
- Wear and tear/increased maintenance to tow vehicle.
- Accomodation costs (unless you camp at the circuit).

Other items that will have to be considered and budgeted for include:
- Possible loss of earnings if injured/insurance costs.
- Contingencies such as damage to the car/engine rebuild.

Working facilities

Assuming that you are intending to prepare and maintain the car at home, you will need a garage that is wide enough for at least one car door to be opened fully and of sufficient length to accommodate the car plus an engine crane, a bench and enough room to work in comfort. In addition, it must also have sufficient space to store spare parts, tyres and tools and, finally, you will presumably want to be able to shut and securely lock the door.

As you are likely to be spending a lot of time in it during the winter months you may wish to be extravagant and arrange for it to be heated, but if you do, try to avoid paraffin or oil burners as these can easily be knocked over. Similarly, any use of heating that involves a naked flame should be avoided as petrol can be spilt or leak, and even a low amount of fumes can ignite easily with catastrophic results.

Adequate lighting and electrical sockets will be needed, the latter preferably situated at both hip and low level on all walls and be capable of being totally turned off from one master switch. The ring main itself should be separate and connected back to the main control box in the house via an MCB (micro circuit breaker), which is a faster and safer alternative to the traditional fuse-box arrangement.

A strong workbench will be required, preferably made of timber, but covered with an aluminium sheet deck that can be wiped clean (steel decking is too slippery). The addition of a vice will instantly lend you another pair of hands, whilst an anglepoise lamp or similar task lighting will also be of benefit, together with a dual electrical socket.

Shelving and cupboard units fixed to the available wall space will provide useful storage and a lockable steel cabinet bolted to the floor will help to prevent your more valuable tools, such as electric drills and sanders, being stolen by a casual thief.

At the risk of sounding like a children's television presenter, start saving all those large ice cream containers as they are useful for storing stripped-down parts and all the nuts and bolts you will gradually accumulate. Similarly, keep any empty oil containers for draining off your old oil that should then be disposed of thoughtfully at the local council tip. Likewise, all those glass jars you would normally throw away can be used for bleeding off brake fluid, for example.

To stop you from having to drip blood onto the clean kitchen floor, it is worthwhile buying a first aid kit to deal with all the cuts and grazes that lie ahead. These kits are available cheaply, can be supplemented as necessary and should contain at least plasters, bandage, tweezers and an eye bath and solution.

There are many opportunities for injury whilst working, suffice to say that you should be as committed to safety in the workshop as you are to performance.

Finally, because you will be working with petrol and other inflammable liquids and a variety of different combustion sources, it is wise to fit a wall-mounted foam or dry powder fire extinguisher. Hopefully it will not be needed, but do not just fit and forget it: familiarize yourself with its operation while you have the chance as later on it may be too late. Also, like the extinguisher fitted in the car, keep an eye on the gauge to check that it is fully charged; they do have a tendency to leak imperceptibly over time.

Tools

Blamed by bad and good workmen alike, cheap tools are not only a waste of money, but dangerous. A hammer imported from the People's Republic of China may appear to be a bargain until the head flies off or explodes in brittle shards. Good tools may seem expensive at first, but if they are looked after well, they will literally last a lifetime. It is rather like buying clothes: three cheap T-shirts rather than one expensive item usually turns out to be a false economy because the colours run, the shirts lose their shape and they end up as rags for the garage. If it is not possible within your budget to buy all of the tools you need from the outset, remember that quality equipment can be built up as needed and when it can be afforded.

After a while, many tools will become instantly recognizable as your own, but this should not deter you from marking them prominently with your name and postcode. Then, should they become mislaid by accident, they are more likely to be returned. It goes without saying that you should be careful about where you leave them: your garage should always be locked securely, and if you need to keep tools in the car, they should be in the boot, out of sight. Always bear in mind how much it would cost to replace your tool collection, and remember that they are usually excluded from most motor and home-insurance policies.

Tools can be stored in a variety of ways from lockable steel cabinets to traditional toolboxes. It is a personal preference, but I find that the plastic 'handyman' trays, which are sold for a pound or two in most DIY stores, are an ideal solution as they contain different sections, have an integral handle and, because they are open, the tools can easily be seen and picked out. They can also be stacked neatly in the car when you go to the circuit (try getting a loaded cabinet in your car).

One disadvantage is that they are not quite large enough for some tools, so there is always the danger that these will be left behind. The solution is to identify these tools separately on a checklist of essential items required for raceday.

The following list is intended as a guide for anyone about to build up a basic toolkit, and so is not exhaustive. As you undertake more work so the number of special tools will increase: there is always the right tool for the job, so try to find it (this is directed to the previous owners of my car, who used open spanners to try to undo difficult nuts and bolts, and so rounded off their edges).

240-volt inspection lamp A lamp with a clip to allow it to be attached to the car is ideal, as is one with a built-in shade or shield to prevent you from being blinded when working. Make sure the cage is sturdy and will not melt from the heat of the bulb.

Trolley jack Big is best, especially the lifting plate, which can then spread the load evenly, safely and prevent damage.

Bottle jack This is useful for jacking-up part of the car or suspension when access is limited.

Axle stands When working beneath the car, never rely upon the jack to support it unless the body is also fully supported by stands: the jack could easily slip or the hydraulics fail, with dire consequences.

Ramps Generally I have never found these as useful as a trolley jack and stands, but they can help to gain limited access to the front or rear of the car.

Socket set (imperial and metric) The ⁵⁄₁₆-⁷⁄₈in and 8-19mm sets are a good start, but larger sizes will be needed as you progress.

Torque wrench When removing and refitting a number of components on a regular basis, it is vital that you qualify the term 'tight'. It is also imperative that specific items, such as engine nuts and suspension components, are tightened in a particular order and to the correct torque.

Adjustable wrench

Molegrips

Spanners Open-ended and ring types will be needed. Try to keep a duplicate set of the commonly used sizes to allow for un/tightening of a nut and bolt from both sides.

Spark plug spanner Always use this or a special socket when changing plugs as they contain a rubber protecting insert to avoid damaging the porcelain insulator.

Brake adjustment spanner If your car is fitted with drum brakes it is likely that you will need to adjust them before each race, due to wear. Therefore, it is important that the correct tool is used as it is less likely to round-off the corners of the adjusting screws.

Set of screwdrivers Assemble the largest number that you can as you will need different sizes of both straight and posidrive type blades for a variety of applications.

Electric drill Preferably two-speed.

12-volt electric drill A rechargeable or hand-drill is ideal for confined spaces and, of course, at the circuit.

Pliers Engineer's and long-nose types.

Wirecutters

Feeler gauge

Test lamp/multimeter

Hacksaw

Files

Craft knife

Wire brush

Ball pein hammer

Grease gun

Oil can

Impact socket set

Blow torch

Foot pump/tyre pressure gauge

Engine hoist

In the paddock

Look around any race paddock during a weekend and you will see a whole range of service vehicles and facilities from the 'tool kit in the boot' to the converted coaches fully fitted out with lights, ramps, electric generators, parasols in the car's livery and so forth. Where you are placed in this array of nomadic service bays will largely be determined by the size of your budget, but whether you are a large or small concern, certain tools and spares will be carried by all. Big may be beautiful, but only if you remember to take it with you.

As well as the main tools listed above you will need certain other items of equipment including:

Gerry cans
Stopwatch
Pitboard

You must also be prepared for breakages and accidental damage, so it is worth building up a supply of spares, the extent of which will depend on your particular discipline, budget and storage capability. It can be just a spare set of points, leads and plugs if you are sprinting your road car, but it may extend to enough spares virtually to build another complete car if you are in a single-seater series or are rallying.

Other considerations

In my first season of circuit racing I had an almost fatalistic approach, none so more evident than in my decision to drive to and from each circuit. Now, as I cruise up the A1 with the air conditioning on, the racecar being towed behind on a double-axle trailer, it makes me wince as I recall my early experiences. During my first season I would think nothing of driving my racecar to far flung circuits, practising, racing, then driving back home – a round trip of 300 miles.

I similarly shudder as I remember one day returning from Brands Hatch with the engine running so badly that I thought it best to ask for a police escort through the Dartford Tunnel in case it gave up the ghost completely. When we later stripped down the engine, one big-end was elliptical and the bearing had long since disappeared.

For sprinting and events requiring little sustained power, I can appreciate the purist's view that the car should be driven to the event, and this makes even more sense if it is your everyday transport. However, for events where the risk of mechanical failure or accident damage is higher, the use of a trailer is essential.

The pros and cons of trailering your car can be summed up as follows:

Advantages
• If you damage the car or it has a mechanical failure such that it cannot be driven, you can still get home.
• Because of the reasoning above, you are less likely to be inhibited in your style of driving: seriously, the thought of getting home does dwell on your mind.
• No road tax is required for the racecar.
• No insurance is required.
• No MoT certificate is required (subject to series regulations).

Disadvantages
• Like restoring a previously well-used sportscar, using a trailer makes you less likely to use your racecar for everyday use on the open road.
• You need a suitable vehicle to tow the trailer (plus, obviously, a tow bar).

• The additional cost of the trailer.
• You need secure space in which to park the trailer.

Advice
You will be faced with a bewildering array of information to take in when you first become a participant in motorsport (consider this book, for instance!) and inevitably much of it will either conflict with or at least not exactly suit your particular situation. It is unfortunate that motor racing, like many sports, has more than its fair share of 'experts', ranging from the armchair racer to the hardened veteran who knows it all. If you take in all the advice you are offered and then make your own decisions, at least you will only have yourself to blame if things go wrong. Everyone else will thus hopefully be spared the whining excuses and attempts to apportion responsibility for your failings to the incompetence of others.

Conclusions
So, having told you that you will need to be rich, with lots of spare time, talent and the loving support of your partner, you could be forgiven if by this stage you were slightly disheartened. "Motor racing is not easy – if it was everyone would do it", is a favourite phrase of a friend of mine and is usually uttered as I sit, head in hands, as another engine smokes expensively in the background. He is right, of course, and within a few hours I have usually recovered the two essentials I have purposely left until last: a sense of humour and enthusiasm. Lose either of these and you may as well pack up.

CHAPTER 3

Secondhand or self-prepared?

"To be successful in racing . . . you need a double motivation: the skills of driving and the skills of organizing and finance."
Ayrton Senna
Sunday Times, July 5, 1987

Many of the monthly car magazines that cater for the club racer and enthusiast regularly feature articles on 'How to become a racing driver', or guidance on 'Racing your road car'. Being enthusiastically written, they provide a good oversight of the sport and are instrumental in motivating their readership.

However, anyone who has been about to undertake a simple task on their car, has consulted the manual and read the frustrating phrase: 'First remove the engine', will know that it is sometimes easy to understate the scale of a problem. With a large budget and access to specialist advice, it is very easy to gloss over the harsh realities of club motorsport, and I sometimes wonder just how many cars have been left to rot unceremoniously once their owners have realized that motor racing is not for them after all. Look in the small ads of the motor racing press and ask yourself why so many cars are being sold, and of these why quite a few are 'part-prepared' or 'abandoned projects'.

What car?

Just as you would be considered foolish if you rushed out and bought the first road car you saw, similarly you should not risk the same sort of mistake when choosing a car that is intended for racing. For instance, do not allow yourself to be persuaded by the appearance of the car as most built for racing have a purposeful air and some can give the impression of speed even when stationary. It is difficult, but essential, to approach the buying process with a cool head, a set of clear objectives and a strict not-to-exceed budget.

For anyone attracted by the prospect of preparing a car from scratch I have one other early word of warning: from an economic standpoint, at the end of the season it is likely that the car will be so specialized as to attract only a limited market, and its resale value will therefore be very low – so low, in fact, that it is quite likely to be far less than the money and effort you have invested in it; in some instances it could even be worth more if broken down into its constituent parts. If you doubt this analogy, consider whether you would buy a road car that had been driven at its limit and had no service record; a car used for racing is potentially even worse. Nevertheless, this does mean that the secondhand values are attractive from a purchaser's viewpoint, a fact that should be weighed-up carefully before you commit yourself to the DIY route.

These rather negative facts are not intended to dissuade you from buying and modifying a road car, but rather to forewarn you to proceed with caution as you will inevitably end up making a financial loss. To the uninitiated, it looks fairly easy to strip out and convert a road car for racing, but what also needs to be taken into account are the many unseen but costly modifications such as engine tuning and suspension uprating which are necessary to guarantee power, reliability and acceptable handling. You also need to place a value on the amount of time spent preparing the car, testing it and carrying out any subsequent modifications. It is rare to be able to bolt on racing versions of standard parts or uprated components and achieve instant and beneficial results from them without further fine tuning.

Another factor you should take into account is that once you have chosen a particular race series to enter, and either bought a car or begun to modify one to suit, it is usually quite costly to change your mind. Even as you make your initial decision as to which discipline to follow, and begin to favour a particular class, you are already reducing your options.

For this reason, great care needs to be taken in choosing the type of racing that best suits you and your particular circumstances, and I would strongly recommend that as a first step you take the trouble actually to go out and watch a number of the different events described in the first chapter.

The key factors that should affect your choice of car include:
• The end use and its suitability for it.
• The level of continuing interest and support for the series in which it is to be raced.
• Its tunability and versatility.
• The time and cost involved in its purchase and preparation.

Buying secondhand
You cannot have too much advice or undertake too much research prior to buying a secondhand race car. Even buying

a road car is difficult enough nowadays, despite the supposed protection of mechanical breakdown insurance and a reliable MoT certificate, so take your time and gather together as much information and guidance as possible before you even start to look for a suitable purchase.

The most reliable source of advice is someone who already owns the type of car you are considering and will therefore know its strengths and weaknesses; try to talk to some of the competitors at different meetings. Another avenue to explore is one or more of the magazines that cater for the club racer; see if they cover the race series or type of racing you are interested in, or have written about the particular model in any of their back issues – these can usually be ordered fairly inexpensively. In addition, if the car concerned has been particularly popular and successful, it may be that a book or two have been published on it, in which case a visit to your main library, one of the specialist bookshops or a racing accessory shop could be helpful.

As for actually locating a suitable car, the classified advertisement section of *Motoring News*, *Autosport* or *Cars and Car Conversions* is probably an ideal place to start. This usually contains a number of advertisements from specialized companies that prepare and deal in racing cars of all types. Private sellers can also be found here advertising cars for all budgets, so from the two types of advertisement you should start to get an idea of price, availability and popularity.

Another potentially useful source of information could be your nearest race accessory shop; they may be able to point you in the direction of known local cars for sale or some specialist dealers in the area worth contacting. However, before you get too rosy a picture of ever-helpful race shop assistants I have to say that although some of them are of the highest quality, in recent times I have encountered a disturbing increase in the number of scowling, pimply youths, who have a tendency to sneer at you no matter how much you are spending and contributing to their being employed. If you do encounter this sort of behaviour, *always* complain to the manager – if enough of us do so perhaps someone will take notice.

Those unmentionables aside, there are some very good companies out there who employ helpful staff, whose advice is available – especially if you are a novice – on such matters as the best type of general equipment to buy, or the tuning potential and special parts available for the model in which you are interested.

When you have completed your homework and are satisfied that an advertised car may be the one for you, telephone the vendor and, from a pre-prepared list, ask as many reasonable questions as you can. These should range from technical specifications through to the car's racing history, but be careful to listen for any non-specific replies and uncertainty. One key question that will require a plausible reply is why is the owner selling the car? Write down all of the information so that you can refer to it later, and conclude with a non-committal statement that you will contact them again should you want to examine the car.

Now comes the difficult part: comparing the details of the car as described with the ideal specification you had in mind and working out whether it still sounds like good value for money. If it seems like a 'probable', telephone back and arrange a convenient time for the car to be viewed, in daylight.

At this stage, if you are mechanically inexperienced you should arrange for the car to be fully examined by someone who knows the potential problems to look for. Also, as touched on earlier, do not rush into buying the first car you see because there may be others that are better, cheaper, or both. The more eligible cars you see the greater your knowledge will become and you will soon be able to identify the common good and bad points, which in turn will help you to negotiate the best deal.

When you view the car it is advisable to check out the following items:

Authenticity

It will probably come as no surprise that the unscrupulous behaviour sometimes found in the motor trade is not confined to the road market. As a prospective purchaser the phrase 'caveat emptor' (buyer beware) should be your motto, as stolen cars can quite easily be transformed into anonymous racers. After all, it does not take a genius to work out that there is no requirement to display a number-plate or be in possession of a registration document for the vehicle as it is not on a public highway. Also, unless it is a specific requirement of the series' technical regulations, you do not even need a current MoT certificate – all of which means that the chances of being detected are remote. After all, when was the last time you saw the Police checking a racing car?

If the car is an ex-road car, whilst the engine identification number may no longer be the original one as a rebuilt unit may have been fitted, there is less excuse for the absence of chassis numbers and you must ask yourself why they have been removed. It may be that the car has been substantially rebuilt, but it could also point to the fact that the rightful owner is still fuming at the loss.

Occasionally, a car will be advertised as having a 'pedigree' that will be reflected in the asking price. It may be claimed, for instance, that the car was a 'works special', or has some other historic significance such as having been raced in the past by a famous driver or in a famous race. In such cases it is important that these facts are verified by checking the relevant details with reference books, motor heritage museums, the original manufacturer, or one of the car clubs that caters for the marque or model in question. The latter group, being enthusiasts, are usually only a telephone call away and will in general only be too happy to share their wealth of knowledge with you. The manufacturers, however, being more commercially-minded, may well be of little or no assistance, so do not expect too much advice from that quarter.

Claims along the lines that the car was driven last year to win a certain championship or achieved so many fastest lap records should be easily confirmed through trophies, official paperwork and photographs which any proud owner will have kept, so beware if these are missing. If any of this documentation is available, ensure that it comes with the car for future use as it will also help you sell the vehicle at a later date. Cynical though it may seem, you should also try to ascertain that the car has not been substantially changed since such exploits.

The whole issue of authenticity is even more critical if you are buying a car for Historic racing or rallying as the qualification criteria are very strict, with homologated parts being checked to ensure that they match contemporary records. If you are buying a car for this specific use you are strongly advised to seek the advice of someone with particular expertise in the marque or model concerned, who can verify whether or not the car is indeed genuine and 'as it left the factory'.

Receipts

Recent and applicable receipts and bills do not just provide proof of the work that has been undertaken and the quality and specification of the fitted parts. They will also help to give a timespan for these elements, plus an indication as to whether they are at the end of their useful life and need replacement. Furthermore, they may well substantiate claims of high-performance engine work, and a useful follow-up if you buy the car is to trace the engine builder, who may recall the handiwork and provide you with further details.

Power and torque curve print-outs from a rolling road should be treated with caution as they are only a record of the engine performance at the time of testing and, as already mentioned, many settings could have changed since then (and possibly even the engine itself). They do provide a useful guide, however, and as stated above any associated documentation and history adds to the car's value.

Quality

It is not possible to provide a definitive checklist for every conceivable aspect of buying a car because to do so would entail another book in itself. Instead, I shall refer to the key areas which you need to examine on a car which has been built for racing.

Whenever you are considering a major purchase of any sort you should be overly concerned for the quality of the product and for the value for money it represents. Two good indications that you are looking at a quality race car seem, at first glance, to be at opposite ends of the spectrum.

The first is the overall impression, which can be a matter of taste, but is normally self-evident in the general presentation of the car. Does it look fit for the purpose, for example? Does it have the appearance of being a well-thought-out project, or are you just looking at the product of a cheap respray and a different set of wheels? Just because the car looks fast it does not mean to say it is not a dog's dinner.

Consider, for instance, the car's age and what it may have already endured on the track and perhaps previously on the road. All cars have known areas that are prone to rusting, so can you be sure that the car you are looking at has not simply been bodged up with filler? That said, there is nothing wrong with an old car as long as it has been repaired or rebuilt where necessary to a proper standard.

At the other end of the scale, the second criterion is to consider the detailed build quality. This will be apparent in areas such as the layout of cockpit instrumentation, the tidiness of the engine bay and the appearance of the paintwork at close quarters. Other key quality indicators include the state of the wiring, especially where new connections have been made into the existing loom or fusebox; 'spaghetti', bare wires, yards of insulating tape are others. Unfortunately, so many cars that convey the external appearance of having been meticulously prepared do not withstand close scrutiny of the electrical system, some even looking as if they have been wired in the dark. Obvious clues like dried rust tidemarks from the last outing when the car overheated, or tell-tale corrosion around the battery terminals, should give you a good indication as to whether the car has been maintained regularly with love and care. Examples such as these should dissuade you almost as much as a recently deposited film of oil coating the engine bay and the underside of the car.

Even if the car is near-perfect, you should still allow a reasonable sum from your budget for an engine and gearbox rebuild to ensure they are what they purport to be and to reassure yourself that they are in good order. This fairly small investment of time spent checking at the beginning may save you considerable trouble and expense later on and at least allow you to start off with a degree of confidence in the power plant. It is also useful for any future development work to be built up from known parameters and a base specification. Unfortunately, inaccurate claims can easily be made about engine components and performance knowing that they cannot be tested on the spot, so a contingency sum needs to be set aside.

Specific physical checks

If the car has been prepared for a particular championship or class it is essential you establish just what those rules are and how the car has been modified to suit. Therefore, detailed research is necessary. Furthermore, if you intend to use the car for a different discipline, for example using a former circuit car for sprints or hillclimbs, you will need to consider the cost of modifications in such areas as engine size, wheels, tyres and suspension.

Check also whether the price includes any spares or useful race equipment. If the vendor is quitting motorsport or moving up to a different category or class, you may be able to haggle for extra items that may no longer be needed.

Even if the car has only completed a single season this is not a guarantee that it has not been 'remodelled', and although any collision damage may have been cosmetically repaired, the chassis or subframes could be substantially weakened or misaligned.

Specific areas to check for any distortion, therefore, include the floorpan and the susceptible crumple zones to the front and rear. The condition of the bodywork will usually be a good reflection of the care and attention the rest of the car has received, and any problems should be self-evident. If there are any special panels, such as nosecones, spoilers or one-piece front sections, check their availability as replacements could be costly.

If you approach any race engine with suspicion and assume it will need to be substantially rebuilt you will not be disappointed. As indicated in the section on receipts, although any background information is helpful, do not place too much reliance on it alone.

Physical checks should be similar to those which are involved when buying a car for the road: check the oil pressure on start-up and when warm, listen for any unusual noises and ensure there are no major oil leaks. Quality should be obvious in the engine bay from the care that has been taken with the wiring and the plumbing for oil and water. Even tiny details are important as they can provide an indication of careful development.

Once you have checked the car thoroughly and have an idea of how much work, if any, you will need to undertake before it is ready to be raced, the final decision on whether to buy it and for how much can only be made by you alone. You will need to weigh up all of the factors mentioned so far, and then balance them against the key one that will enable the deal to be clinched: the price.

Generally, I would recommend setting aside at least 10 to 20 per cent of your budgeted purchase price for any additional work that may be necessary, and if you do all your homework and haggle over the asking price you may end up with this anyway.

Another factor to be considered is that secondhand race cars are quite a specialized area and therefore a prospective car is unlikely to be snapped up immediately. So take your time and always be prepared to bargain.

Preparing your own car
Preparing a car rather than buying one secondhand is an attractive option for a variety of reasons, including being able to build it to your own specification and therefore to rest a little easier with the assurance that the quality of components and workmanship meets your own exacting standards.

Upon completion, which is usually some time after the date originally planned, you should also be able to enjoy the satisfaction of having carried out the work yourself. As hinted at the beginning of this chapter, however, the DIY option is rarely likely to pay for itself in terms of the final value of the car when completed; although it may cover the sum spent on the components, the build time and any associated labour costs will normally be lost.

Before plunging headlong into the project there is one significant theme which should accompany all of your car preparation: the need for safety. It is a fact that when complete, your car will be expected to carry you at high speeds on the extreme edge of your driving abilities with an ever-present risk of an accident that will be either your fault, that of another driver, or simply down to bad luck. The latter two areas are difficult to influence, but your own situation is one over which you alone have control. If you take this logic a stage further and accept that an accident can be attributed to either the driver or the car, by recognizing the need to make the car as safe as possible you will be improving your odds considerably at a stroke. Do not be mistaken into thinking that all you are doing is modifying a road car to go quicker.

Having said that, if your existing road car is suitable for modification, this is a good way to start in motorsport as it is cheap as well as being attractive to like-minded enthusiasts. Obviously, by using your normal everyday transport you will avoid the extra capital cost of another dedicated car, you will not have to worry about where to store it, you will avoid the need for a trailer and so on.

As your racing progresses, though, you will realize that competition and everyday usage do not sit very well together and that comfort must eventually cede to the demands of racing performance. In the normal production classes at sprints, hillclimbs and autotests you can generally get away with using a standard car, but in modified classes, or when circuit racing, a dedicated vehicle is needed if you are to have any hope of being even modestly successful. So, although the thought of racing your road car at famous circuits is appealing, the prospect of the journey to and from the circuit in a stripped-out noisy monster that refuses to pull below 4,000 revs tends to make the idea less attractive.

Similarly, you also have to consider how you will get home if the car is sufficiently damaged or suffers a mechanical failure to render it undriveable.

If the idea of preparing another car to your own specification appeals, a completely different set of criteria applies when you are searching for a suitable donor car to be modified, although many of the points covered earlier regarding buying a prepared car are also relevant. The possibility of short or medium-term obsolescence needs to be assessed, or you will be spending time and effort working on a car without having a race class or series in which to compete. It is essential, therefore, to choose a model that is widely supported and has a reliable and stable future on the race scene.

The concept of racing an exotic sportscar will need to be weighed against cost, but you do not necessarily have to settle for a mass-produced model. Steadily, over the past few years, 'hot hatches' and other high-performance cars have attracted equally high insurance premiums, so their prices have fallen dramatically, and as insurance is not a mandatory factor on a race track they can be quite an attractive proposition.

Once you have decided on the exact make and model and have been able to concentrate on specific cars within your budget, various sources are available for locating a suitable donor car for racing: the scrapyard, advertisements in shop windows, local newspapers, national and local trade marts to name just some of them. Here are a few of the important factors to consider when looking:

• The car must be the correct model and year for the class in which you wish to compete. This is particularly relevant in the growing Historic racing and rallying competitions, but applies equally to those race series in which organizers try to keep costs down by restricting them to cars over a certain age.

• Do not buy a pristine-looking car as this will be reflected in the price. Instead, you should concentrate on trying to find a sound car, preferably painted in a solid primary colour (avoid metallics if possible) that is easy to match when the inevitable body repair work is needed. Also, remember that beige racing cars are not the norm.

• Similarly, do not be concerned about the state of the interior as the first job will be to strip it out. If it is in good condition, try to sell it – every little bit helps.

• Avoid cars whose price reflects a new or reconditioned engine as you will soon be replacing it.

• On the other hand, and for the same reason, a 'non-runner' is not a problem, especially if the price is right.

• Equally, a damaged but repairable car from a salvage or breakers yard is also a viable option if the damage is to areas where you would be undertaking work anyway. If the car has been stolen and recovered it may be incomplete, for example the trim and seats may have been removed. As above, this is an ideal situation as these items are not required. If you are considering buying a car that has only been in a light accident, bear in mind that it may nevertheless have sustained damage to the chassis or subframes and weakened parts of the structure that you will be subjecting to additional abnormal stresses on the track. In this respect you cannot be too careful.

All cars may be different, but each will require the same basic modifications and preparation to make them safe. The main guidelines for ensuring this are set out in the RACMSA *Blue Book*, which is updated annually, and the latest edition of which you will have received when you applied for your competition licence. If you have not yet applied, try to borrow a copy from someone who already has one, or better still, order one from the RACMSA.

The first part to consult on car preparation is the technical section in the chapter entitled 'Common regulations for competitors' which, as the name suggests, sets out basic criteria from construction through to silencing. Additional requirements are then set out in chapters for each race discipline, in our case 'Specific regulations for car racing', which again contains a dedicated technical section. These are then followed by 'Formulae regulations' that detail the specific requirements for the more popular classes of car racing. Confused? Well, it is fairly complicated, but there again, so is the subject matter, and it does become clearer the more you read it and apply it to your own situation. Consequently, I do not propose to paraphrase it as to do so would not do justice to its detail, besides which, you would not forgive me for any omissions. Instead, in the next two chapters I offer some additional hints and tips to complement some of the regulatory aspects, and hopefully these will prove to be of practical value in their application. The first concentrates on the elementary preparations needed for all circuit cars, and the chapter following explores how to make the car perform better rather than just simply just comply with the rules.

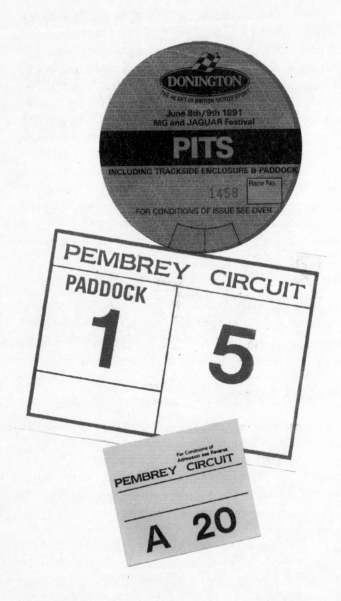

CHAPTER 4

Basic car preparation

"The talent required to drive a machine to the ultimate of its ability is the same; the same inherent chemical element is present today as when the sport began. Machines need to be interpreted and understood."
Jackie Stewart
Sunday Times, August 21, 1983

The car's performance and integral safety will be directly affected by the standard of work and care taken during its preparation. If this work is carried out to the highest possible level you should not only benefit from better results, but also improved reliability and – equally important – increased confidence. Although meticulous attention to detail in car preparation can be very time-consuming, it can actually save time in the long run by avoiding the need for further work such as having to replace imperfect items at the most inconvenient of times – perhaps even during a race meeting. Therefore, you should consider the whole subject of car preparation as an investment rather than as just a means to an end. As proof of the value of this advice, I am honest enough to admit that I have had cause to regret not having taken it – usually when my efforts have been thwarted by the failure of a temporary or running repair (otherwise known as a 'bodge').

The main areas on which to concentrate include the following:

Chassis/structure
The chassis or overall structural frame of a race car does not need integral strength just to withstand the possibility of collision or accident damage. Rigidity is also required to ensure that the car does not flex or bend under the severe loadings imposed by cornering, braking and accelerating forces, and to provide a stable platform for the suspension. If the car is being distorted physically this will result in the suspension having to work unnecessarily to compensate and, in the worst case, it could give the impression that the car is driving you because of its sloppy, imprecise handling giving the feeling of it being off-balance. Even if the car's structure is distorting only slightly this will be reflected in slower lap times, and you may be unaware of the problem, perhaps blaming the tyres, the suspension, or even yourself instead. You can console yourself with the fact that a brilliant driver may make a bad car look mediocre, but will find it very difficult to win with it.

Continual flexing and twisting will also tend to concentrate loadings on the weaker elements of the car as acceleration, braking and cornering forces will be imposed on the chassis to a greater degree. This is even more prevalent in rallying, where the car is also subjected to severe punishment from rough terrain, but it can apply equally to a circuit car fitted with slick tyres, the phenomenal grip of which results in suspension points being subjected to even greater loads.

All of this can result in stress fractures, which are hairline cracks and can appear at points of weakness such as chassis junctions, body panel welds, suspension fixing points, the turrets at the top of shock-absorbers or the rear spring hangers.

It is unfortunate, but these areas are the most susceptible to corrosion, and rust will be evident in some form or another in most road cars over five years old unless you are very lucky. Depending on the particular model, corrosion could be anywhere, but the common areas are sills, floors and inner arches and anywhere else where water and salt can do its evil work. It is not uncommon to have to cut out whole floorpans and replace them – so be prepared.

Your first task, therefore, is to strip out all the carpets and unnecessary trim and inspect for evidence of stress cracks and corrosion. This is also the best time to remove any underseal or sound-deadening material used to dampen the drumming effect of large panels as this is all extra weight. At first, you may be sceptical as to whether such measures really have an effect, but you will probably change your mind as the plastic bag you use to collect the chiselled debris gradually becomes heavier.

Badly rusted areas should be cut out and replaced, with additional strengthening plates as necessary welded back in. Even if no hairline cracks are found from a close inspection it is still a good idea at this early stage to run a line of weld along the internal junctions of chassis or body panels. This process, known as seam welding, is a laborious job, but it ensures that the chassis and bodywork will act monolithically and that any loads and stresses will be equally distributed.

By now you should have considered the type and design of rollcage that will best suit your application and, once satisfied with the soundness of the overall structure, it will be necessary to locate and weld-in the additional strengthening plates that will be needed to spread the load from its feet and connection points to the bodyshell. If possible, these plates should be fabricated larger than the 120sq cm minimum requirement so as to spread the load more effectively, thereby minimizing the possibility of the rollcage feet in particular from punching through or tearing out should the car be rolled badly. Wherever possible, these plates should also be right-angled and welded to another plane of the bodywork such as the inner sill, as this increases the strength substantially.

One of your final welding tasks should be to fit projecting towing eyes to the front and rear of the car if these are not already in place. These can be welded to the existing towing points, and to give you an idea of strength required, they should be robust enough, at worst, to enable a tow truck to pull the car diagonally from a gravel trap. Once fitted they should be painted in a contrasting colour to the body so that they can be found easily in an emergency, and their position should be clearly marked on the front and rear valances by the word 'tow' or an arrow.

Rollcages

If you consider that you may be unfortunate enough to be involved in a collision that could be the equivalent of crashing a light aircraft, it becomes imperative to ensure that you are adequately protected. Your rollcage should therefore be specifically designed and fabricated for your precise model of car, and care should be taken to ensure that it fits well.

From a safety aspect, the rollcage should be just that and, despite the minimum safety requirements identified in the *Blue Book* or in the series regulations, much more than simply a single rollbar – leave such decorations to sporty jeeps. Not only will the cage protect you, but it will also, for example, limit damage to the shell and panels should the car roll, so try to make it fit as closely to the internal bodywork as possible. Each year there tend to be rumours that rollcage metal thicknesses are about to be increased, so prior to purchase it is advisable to check whether or not the standards are to be raised.

Most cars are catered for in the product ranges of the rollcage manufacturers, but before you order, consider the merits of fitting additional door bars for side impact protection – these are mandatory if the doors are lightened – and diagonal or lateral bracing, especially between the rear wheelarches, to link each side of the car. If you are also intending to use the car on the road it may be worthwhile considering fitment of removable diagonals and door bars as they can be a considerable hindrance when trying to carry passengers. Note that if you modify or weld additional material to a rollcage this may well render its homologation guarantee invalid, so you must bolt-on, rather than weld-in, any additional tubes, although if contemplating any modifications it is worthwhile checking with the original manufacturer.

Rollcages used to be considered as the primary means of protecting the driver should the car overturn, but they are now valued additionally for their contribution to rigidity, as already mentioned. The rollcage should therefore be considered as an integral part of the car to the extent that in some cases many areas of the bodywork can become redundant. This multi-point or spaceframe system allows high loads to be picked up at specific points – notably where the suspension is connected – and redistributed through the rollcage frame, thus reducing any concentrated stresses.

To increase the car's rigidity as much as possible you should try to triangulate the cage, the principle being, as the name suggests, to design the bracing in order to form triangles, which have more inherent strength. It may also be prudent to fit a strut brace, which spans across the engine bay between the front dampers and thus minimizes movement in this area; if this can also be linked back into the main rollcage so much the better.

On a scale of the world's most difficult tasks, fitting a full rollcage, despite the simple accompanying instructions, lies somewhere between childbirth and getting a ship into a bottle. In order to make it easier you should remove all of the seats and enlist the assistance of someone with patience. Once the frame has been assembled in the car try to push each leg outwards as near to the body as possible before they are bolted down. This will put the cage into tension and help you to fix additional studs linking the uprights to the door pillars. As in the seam welding process, the key to success is connecting the cage to the main structure of the car so that it all acts monolithically.

All parts of the cage that are capable of coming into contact with any part of the driver – and navigator, if rallying – should be covered with non-flammable padding, which does not mean plumber's pipe-lagging but proper high-density foam. This should be fitted securely to the rollcage with cable ties rather than tank tape, which tends to lose its adhesion after a while and causes it to come loose, usually at the worst possible moment.

Bodywork
The standard bodywork of most road cars is suitable for the race track providing certain commonsense safety modifications have been carried out. Glass windscreens must be of the laminated type, now fitted as standard to most modern cars, and this can be verified by checking the British Standard kitemark in one corner.

Glass sunroofs, whether laminated or not, are expressly forbidden, so they need to be either replaced with a metal blanking-plate or removed and a piece of sheet metal welded or pop-riveted over the aperture.

As most racing occurs during the summer months it can get very hot inside, especially after the car has been sitting on the grid for a while, so fitting a net to the inside of the opening will allow the window to be open yet prevent your arm or head from falling out, which is a sobering thought.

Standard door handles and lock mechanisms can remain, but it is advisable to disengage the interior lock buttons in case they get activated and prevent you from exiting the car in the event of an accident. The bonnet and hatchback catches/locks should be removed and replaced with safety fasteners to enable them to be opened quickly in the event of a fire. Different types of fastener are available and choice is down to personal preference, but from experience, the stretched rubber toggles are only suitable for a tailgate and even then they occasionally raise eyebrows during scrutineering. As the bonnet is always in the way when you are removing or fitting the engine you may wish to replace the hinge arrangement with fasteners at the same time, allowing it to be removed completely; this also marginally saves weight.

Finally, all loose trim, bezels and items such as wheel embellishers and chrome strips should be removed as they can be lethal objects at speed; the main headlamps and any auxiliary foglamps should be taped to the bodywork so that if they break they will hold together in one piece and not cause a hazard on the track.

Seats
In an environment where concentration is paramount and any physical discomfort will be an unwelcome distraction, you owe it to yourself to be both comfortable and secure, and your choice of seat will influence this.

It should be a sturdy, single-piece seat, incapable of tilting or hinging, and manufactured by a company with an established reputation. Unsurprisingly, there is a marked difference between cheap seats and seats that have been built cheaply, so examine the quality carefully. As weight may be a factor you should consider the type of seat materials accordingly as many are made in glass/carbon-fibre or Kevlar, the latter being the lightest and strongest option, albeit the most expensive.

The phrase 'driving by the seat of your pants' is a truism and before purchase you should always try out the seat for size and comfort, paying particular attention to how it holds you at the hip and upper body. Try to avoid seats that are padded excessively, however, as although they may be comfortable they can detract from the firmness and 'feel' you should get through the seat. Also check whether the integral head restraint area projects high enough as in a collision it may have to absorb the combined travelling force of your head and helmet to prevent whiplash injuries. If there is no restraint or it is too low, you must fit a padded one to the rollcage diagonal or hoop for this purpose. Finally, the seat should have sufficient slots to accommodate the lap and shoulder harnesses, but also may have additional ones in the base to enable a full harness to be fitted, as detailed below.

Most seats come without a subframe, which will need to be bought separately, but depending on the arrangement in your car it may be simpler and stronger to make up the height by bolting the seat down on to steel or aluminium angles fitted to the existing seat anchorage points or directly through the floor. If the latter is done, make sure it is strengthened and a spreader-plated fitted.

When you are trying to decide the exact position of the seat, remember that as a rule most seats in road cars are offset from the centre to give the impression of a spacious interior. You will therefore benefit ergonomically by positioning the new seat such that its centre aligns directly with the brake pedal. Vertically, in order to help lower the effective centre of gravity of the car, the seat should be as low as possible while still allowing you to see out; as you will be wearing a helmet this will also ensure that you have adequate headroom. A good example of a low seating position is provided by that in Jo Winkelhock's BMW touring car, which appears to be so low as to warrant a booster cushion, yet does not appear to affect his driving abilities.

If you fit a seat that slides forwards and backward to suit the driver, once you are satisfied with the position it is advisable to lock the sliding mechanism both to disable it and to reduce the free play in the runners. A simple tip to achieve this is to fit jubilee clips at each corner and tighten them up once you are happy with the position.

Lastly, although a white leather seat may look smart in the showroom, be practical and pick one that is predominantly dark to conceal dirt and grease stains, preferably in a material that can be cleaned easily.

Harnesses
All of the racing disciplines require full harnesses, as opposed to normal seat belts, to be fitted and it is worth buying at least a four-point set, or a six-point if your seat has a slot in the base. If you are so reclined as to be virtually lying back in your seat, as is common in all single-seaters, these additional straps are vital to prevent you slipping under the lap belt if the car stops suddenly in an accident. Known as submarining, this phenomenon has been widely recognized for many years, yet it is surprising to see some competitors to be still at risk in this respect.

When selecting a suitable type of harness from the many available, pick one that has webbing at least three inches wide with an aero-type or quick-release centre buckle. Additional shoulder pads can also be bought to prevent chafing, but those provided with most harnesses are adequate already. Also, before you buy, be sure to check the manufacturer's details to see if eyebolts are included or need to be purchased separately.

When fitting, it is usually sufficient to remove the existing seat-belt bolts at either side of the seat and fit the new eyebolts in their place, unless you wish to be able to remove the harness and retain the existing seat belts for day-to-day use, when additional holes will have to be drilled. For the fixing points at the rear you may be able to use the existing threaded holes used for fitting rear seat belts, but check that the angles are satisfactory.

Any new fixing points should be to a part of the car that is strong and not too thin, otherwise the fixings could rip out, so additional welded plates may be required. However, do not be tempted to fit the straps to the rollcage or any side panelling as in an accident these could distort or buckle, causing the straps to tighten, restricting your chest, preventing you breathing and perhaps inflicting injury. The correct adjustment of your harness is covered later.

Fire precautions

A fire is more likely to occur in a race car than in a standard road car as, of course, the risk of collision is greater, the fuel is likely to be under greater pressure and the original wiring will have been subject to modification. In less than a minute an engine fire can at best ruin all of your hard work and at worst kill you, so the whole issue of fire, from prevention through to limitation and extinguishing, needs to be respected and made an integral part of your car preparation.

On standard road cars the engine bay, as a high fire risk, is separated from the rest of the car by a metal bulkhead to hold back the initial smoke and flames, thereby enabling the car to be stopped and the occupants to climb out. If you have ever witnessed a car fire you will know that the time for it to spread from the bay to the rest of the car is a matter of minutes due to the holes in the bulkhead and the melting of the rubber grommets that seal penetrations.

As you will be making these holes bigger when you remove extraneous wiring looms and the heater ducting or form/drill additional ones, the eventual integrity of the bulkhead is critical. Large openings should be blanked off with pop-riveted steel sheet, any smaller gaps and imperfections being filled with intumescent putty/mastic, which is available from builders' merchants.

Extinguishers need to be fitted to all cars, the current minimum requirement being a small 2.5kg hand-operated type, which is generally adequate for small cars competing in timed events such as autotests or sprints. If you are fitting this type, remember to locate it within reach when you are strapped into your race harness, either in the footwell area or secured to the rollcage upright. Wherever you fix the extinguisher, make sure it is secured safely: you will hear many a tale of them becoming loose and bouncing alarmingly around the footwell. A useful tip is to fit a brightly coloured ribbon or piece of tape to the disarming pin to remind you to remove it when competing.

For events such as circuit racing or rallying, where there is more risk of fires occurring and on a more damaging scale, extinguishers with a greater capacity are required and ideally a plumbed-in system should be fitted. These larger sizes of extinguisher can either discharge simultaneously into the engine bay and the cockpit or, if two systems are installed, serve those areas separately. Operated either electrically or mechanically, their main advantage is one of total coverage, plus the ability for them to be activated within the car or externally by a marshal, which is comforting to know as you may be unconscious or trapped upside down at the time.

All extinguishers should be fitted with a gauge to indicate that they are full, but it is worth having it weighed properly at the end of each season and recharged if necessary. If the car is not to be used for any length of time, such as in the winter, it is advisable to remove the extinguisher and store it vertically as the steel case can corrode where it rests on the floorpan. Similarly, the joint between the aluminium head and the case can be susceptible to light corrosion and leakage, so this area should also be checked.

Due to the detrimental effects of CFC gases on the environment, Halon or BCF-filled extinguishers are to be phased out from January 1, 1996 and replaced by less harmful, alternative extinguishants. Therefore, if you are offered a cheap extinguisher in the meantime, check it carefully in case it is of the type about to be discontinued.

The fuel tank of a car that previously has been used on the road may have corroded, especially if it has been exposed on the underside, so it should be examined very carefully. If you are retaining the existing tank it is worthwhile removing it and having it cleaned out thoroughly as over the years it is likely to have accumulated sludge, grit and rust flakes, which will be disturbed as soon as you get on the track; you should also consider fitting an in-line fuel filter. Looking at other cars in the paddock, you will see that many tanks have been replaced, perhaps with one in a lighter aluminium and relocated in a more central and therefore balanced position.

Generally, tanks and fuel lines should be positioned away from any immediate impact area and protected from stones or other flying debris that may be thrown up onto the underside of the car. Tanks should be fitted with a sealed cap and spill tray as well as be vented to the open air. The vent tube should be sealed off from the inside of the car and preferably fitted with a non-return valve to prevent spillage should the car overturn. All fuel lines should be of the Aeroquip type, secured to the bodywork out of the way of the exhaust and, if run inside the car, of one length to minimize the risk of leaks.

Electrics

It is vitally important when you are preparing a car for racing that the electrical system is in good condition to help guarantee reliability and that you are safe from short-circuits that could cause a fire. When modifying a road car, it is wise to take out any fuses to items no longer required such as the cigar lighter, and remove all extraneous cabling, taking care to insulate effectively any bare wires. Similar care should be taken when connecting new items, ensuring that they are connected through the fusebox and the fuses are correctly rated. Removing all the wiring you do not need is time-consuming, but it will decrease the risk of short-circuits and make any new wiring connections easier to secure.

In an accident, in order to turn off the engine and isolate all electrical circuits – thereby reducing the risk of fire – an in-line circuit breaker switch, capable of being operated both inside and outside the car has to be fitted. This can involve wiring two switches in-line, or more commonly, a switch on the dashboard also operable by a cable-pull located in front of the windscreen, preferably on the driver's side. The external switch should be clearly marked with a red flash on a blue triangle and both should indicate their 'on' and 'off' positions. When choosing a position for the external isolator switch, make sure it does not foul the bonnet if this is hinged and that it will not be adversely affected by water penetration.

If the alternator is being retained, it is important to wire in the switches so that it is isolated or will continue to supply electricity to the engine even if the battery has been disconnected. Also, because the alternator diodes can easily be damaged by current surges, make sure that you fit the correct type of switch of the two types available.

The battery should preferably be of a non-maintained type, strapped firmly in place to prevent it moving around when you are driving and, if the regulations allow, it should be repositioned so that it is less susceptible to damage in a collision. Wherever sited, both battery terminals should be fitted with plastic insulating covers, particular care being taken with the positive one as in a collision the bonnet could distort and be bent so as to touch it, causing a short-circuit. If the battery is to be relocated within the car itself, it should be contained in a purpose-made sealed box which will prevent spillage and fumes. Finally, the negative earth wire should be easily distinguishable by being coloured yellow (to enable it to be identified and cut in an emergency). As paint rarely dries well on rubber and plastic, wrapping it with the appropriate coloured insulating tape is the easiest way of doing this.

Engine

The *Blue Book* makes various references to the engine and its ancillaries, many of which are simply common sense. Particular requirements that are easy to forget, however, include the need for an additional positive method of closing the throttle should the linkage fail and cause the car to go out of control. This can be achieved by connecting another spring; do not try to argue with the scrutineer that there are already two springs to most throttle linkages, just fit it.

Another special requirement is the need for an oil catch tank to be connected to the engine's breather tubes so that should the engine 'blow' it will not spill oil over the track (in a road car these breathers are usually connected back into the engine through the carburettor). The best catch tanks are purpose-made of aluminium, with a clear sight gauge, although another cheaper but effective alternative is to use a translucent radiator expansion tank suitably plugged at the base and liberally drilled with holes on top. This additional ventilation is essential to prevent the crankcase from becoming pressurized, leading to poor performance and oil leaks at weak points in the engine (usually at the junction of the engine/gearbox). For this same reason you should periodically check and clean the internal bores of the breather pipes – fitting the largest possible size is also preferable.

Another aspect you should consider is minimizing engine movement as this not only stresses the engine mounts and any pipes or wiring, but in cars with transverse engines or remote gear selectors, it can even prevent gearchanges at high engine speeds. Although you may think the engine is relatively solid and cannot be rocked by hand, this is disproved if you ever watch the way it bucks and twists on a car that is being taken up through the gears on a rolling road.

The first step to limit engine movement is to fit uprated mounts – or even solid replacements if you do not mind the noise and are prepared for the chassis being subjected to additional stresses – followed by fitting an adjustable engine-steady bar between the engine and the body/chassis.

Ready to race
One piece of advice which you will ignore at your cost is the well-known racing adage: "To finish first, first you must finish." This phrase is one that most club racers will become accustomed to hearing during their first season and which you too will probably recall with chagrin on your first encounter with unreliability.

All of the work described so far has been necessary to ensure that the car is safe in an emergency situation, or to prevent such a situation occurring, but other modifications will also be needed because of the very nature of racing.

Instrumentation
In modern road cars, instruments such as the tachometer or oil pressure gauge are becoming rare in all but the sport or prestige models. Instead, the driver relies on warning lights

should the engine temperature become too hot or the oil level drop too low, for instance.

This move away from dashboards that look like jet-fighter flight decks can mainly be attributed to changing styles, lower overall production and maintenance costs, but also convenience. With busy lifestyles that demand fast convenience foods and cars, who wants the burden of having to cosset the car? The increased reliability and sophistication of engines helps as the driver does not need to monitor performance and warning signals, the car's engine management system doing it automatically and alerting the driver as necessary.

In a car built for racing, this minimalist philosophy also holds true – the driver does not want to keep looking at gauges when there is so much else going on to command the attention. Instruments should therefore be kept to a minimum and the emphasis instead be placed on warning lights to alert the driver of problems. Having said this it is important that those instruments and sensors are accurate and superior to the standard road car versions. When the low oil pressure light comes on it is also important to be able to check whether you have 25psi or nothing at all. It therefore makes sense to replace critical switches and senders with uprated versions that will be more reliable and accurate.

There may be certain gauges that are applicable to your car, to record boost for instance if you are running a turbo, but the essential ones needed by all cars include:

A tachometer A tip is to overmark the dial face with the engine's effective power band to let you know the optimum point to change gears. Although more expensive, there are also types that have a built-in playback facility so that you can analyze your gearchanges after the race or testing to try to maximize your performance. See also the reference to the gearchange light later.

Oil pressure gauge This is a good indicator of the health of the engine. On starting up, it will give its highest reading, but after a race, when the engine is idling, the pointer may drop alarmingly. This is due to the thin viscosity of the hot oil, and is quite normal as long as it generally reads over 20psi. If it is less than this, however, you are likely to have worn engine bearings that will soon need replacing.

Oil temperature gauge All engines have an ideal temperature range within which they are working at their peak performance, and this usually lies between 70 and 80deg C. If the engine is hotter than this it will overheat, cause the coolant to boil and potentially blow the head gasket; if it is too cool the engine will be inefficient and suffer greater wear. For this reason you should never race the car before the engine has been warmed up properly.

Water temperature gauge In conjunction with the above this will monitor the coolant temperature and indicate whether the correct operating temperature has been reached or is being exceeded.

Fuel gauge You will not want to carry too much fuel as it is all extra weight, but conversely you do not want to run out. The best way to make sure your gauge is accurate is to empty the tank and then mark the dial after you have poured in measured amounts. Do remember, however, that for all this accuracy the petrol will be slopping all over the place and, depending on the orientation of the sender unit, it could be giving a false reading. The only way to solve this problem is to note the way it reads during practice whilst cornering and see if it becomes more accurate on a straight. Also, do not forget the common practice of calculating your predicted fuel consumption to the nearest decimal place and then adding an extra 5 litres to be on the safe side!

You may note that I have deliberately omitted the speedometer from the list of instruments as it is both irrelevant on a race track and liable to worry you unnecessarily. You do not need the sight of a speedo needle bending off the dial, believe me.

Gauges should be backed up by the following warning lights:

Battery charge/Ignition on This will warn you if the engine has stalled or that the alternator, if fitted, is not charging the battery. It may be that the fan belt is loose or has come off completely, so keep an eye on the temperature gauge as the water pump may not be working.

Low oil pressure As mentioned earlier, in the heat of the moment it is unlikely that you will notice the loss of oil pressure until it is too late, so a large orange lamp – a side indicator lamp is ideal – in a prominent position will possibly save your engine. It is also practical to fit an oil pressure switch that will cut power to the electric fuel pump should the pressure drop too low.

Handbrake warning lamp It would not do to have to blame your poor performance on your forgetting to let the handbrake off, would it?

If you have modified a road car, many of the warning lights for choke, indicators and so on, can be left, but if you are replacing the dashboard many can be discarded from your new layout. The layout of any instruments in a new dashboard or binnacle is important – try to fit the tachometer centrally with the most commonly-used gauges immediately adjacent. A trick used in the aviation industry is to orientate the gauges so that the needles are vertical when giving a normal reading, which allows your eyes to scan them quickly and immediately identify any discrepancy. Other controls that you will need to consider include:

• An override switch for the electric cooling fan if fitted.

• Light switches because whilst you will not normally be driving in the dark, if it becomes wet or overcast dipped headlights will help you to be noticed by slower cars ahead. Indicators are not required, but working brakelights and rearlights are mandatory and will often be checked at scrutineering.

• Windscreen wiper and washer controls – easily overlooked, but essential as, by the law of averages, some of your racing will be on a wet track. Without them you will be faced with having to peer through the spray ahead of you. Your car may be the fastest, but it will be impotent if you cannot see where you are going. The rear wiper, if fitted, is worthless and only contributes extra weight so it can be removed, whereas front wipers can be reduced to just a single arm and blade. Replace any large washer reservoir bottle with one that is smaller – it may still be needed if the screen becomes smeared with oil and dust, especially if it also rains.

• A gearchange light. Now cheaply available, this is a useful driver aid that consists of a small box housing an electronic circuit connected to the coil and a red lamp. When the engine reaches an adjustable pre-set speed, say 7,000rpm, the lamp flashes to indicate that you are at the top of the engine's power band and should change up a gear. A further development is to have another light flashing on when the revs have dropped to a pre-set figure at the bottom of the known power band, thus advising you to change down a gear. Whether you are comfortable with your dashboard lighting up like a Christmas tree is down to personal preference.

Steering wheel

There are many after-sale steering wheels and boss adaptors suitable for your car, of all sizes, designs and costs. Generally, you need to buy one smaller than fitted as standard, but do not be tempted to buy one that is so ridiculously small that it is heavy to steer around sharp corners. In addition, do not buy one with a wooden rim as these can splinter lethally in an accident, and avoid those wheels that have sharp raised bolts at the centre, for obvious reasons. Once the wheel is fitted, a final practical tip is to mark the top with a brightly coloured piece of insulating tape: if you spin or slide it is useful when recovering to have some indication of the normal steering position.

You should ensure that the steering lock is disengaged and preferably removed altogether to prevent it accidentally becoming operational when racing, with disastrous results. Ideally you should replace the assembly by wiring in a simple but robust on/off switch to make the ignition live, together with a pushbutton to turn the starter motor. This arrangement also has the benefit of allowing you to turn the engine over and build up oil pressure before finally making the ignition live and starting it up. Note that, like the main battery isolator, the switch will have to be marked clearly.

Footwell

On secondhand cars of any age it is likely that the pedals will have excess travel that should be adjusted at their stop ends to make the controls more efficient. You should pay particular attention to the accelerator pedal stop as, if it is not adjusted correctly, your exuberant right foot can easily snap the throttle cable. When making adjustments to the stop, try to make the accelerator pedal height level with that of the brake pedal when depressed. If this can be done it will make it easier to change your right foot quickly from one pedal to the other.

Normal road use requires pedals to be quite spaced apart whereas for racing it is preferable for them to be closer as the lesser the distance the quicker they can be operated, but do not make them so close that you cannot distinguish between them. Offset additional plates are available which can be fixed to provide wider non-slip surfaces and reduce the distances accordingly.

While you are working on this area it is a good idea to fit a footrest immediately to the left of the clutch pedal. As well as discouraging you from riding the clutch, it can also be used to brace against and push your body well back into the seat prior to clipping the harness. Finally, do not forget to fit a chequer-plate or secure a rubber mat in the footwell to stop your heels from slipping if wet. For this reason, if it has been raining, it is also helpful to keep a small piece of clean rag handy to wipe your shoes dry.

Ventilation

In a move designed to shed weight, the heater box with its fan, matrix and controls is often the first object to be discarded from a road car. Unfortunately, this also removes the ability to demist the windscreen – which many drivers have discovered to their cost when it rains or during practice on a crisp morning – and to ensure a comfortable flow of air through the car.

There are two common and successful methods of combating the problem of a misting windscreen: fitting a long piece of flexible pipe – such as that found on a vacuum cleaner – between the existing screen and the leading edge of the bonnet in the engine bay, which will then push cool air onto the screen as the car moves; or fitting a 12-volt hairdrier, of the type presumably used by image-conscious caravanners, to the existing screen duct, with a conveniently placed in-line switch. The latter is the better solution as it does not rely on the car moving and the heating element will help to clear the windscreen more quickly.

In order to ensure adequate ventilation in the car, a window net has already been described, but another method is to use the ducting idea again and terminate a flexible tube on top of the steering column or on the door pillar, pointing at your face. Please be careful, however, to ensure that any ducting that passes through the engine bay is suitably shielded or insulated from any fire that may occur.

The best place to start any motorsports career: the RAC 'Blue Book' is the essential reference for all competitors and should be studied scrupulously.

Sprinting is an ideal stepping-stone to circuit racing and whether you run a Cobra or a Mini it can be one of the cheapest forms of the sport.

Hill-climbing is another option, requiring great accuracy to avoid suspension-unsettling verges and unyielding walls.

Paddock Bend at Brands Hatch is one of the big thrills of UK racing, especially if you are in the middle of a pack of identical Renaults.

The racing can sometimes be even closer with a mixed bag of saloons and marque rivalry adding spice to the human contest. The secret is not to become flustered.

To go racing you need a car, some kit and – equally important – some friends; even if they're ugly you'll find you can't do without them. Here are two of mine, doing their best to dent the Metro.

Of course, spinning into the Armco and coming back with scarred panelwork and dangling extensions is enough to take the smiles off their faces.

It helps if your pit crew can count because what they put on your pit board can influence how you run your race, and even where you finish.

Even for the best-prepared car there is bound to be work to do in the paddock, even if it is just removing the wheels and checking and cleaning off the brakes.

Sometimes, practice will reveal a more serious problem, in which case a well-trained crew, who really know your car inside-out, can perform near-miracles in the brief time before your race.

The first step to a well-prepared car is a top-quality toolkit. This is an area where buying top-quality but premium-price tools can actually save you money in the long run.

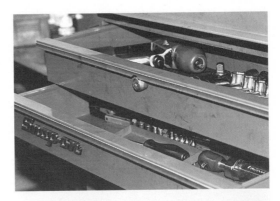

A visit to a rolling road run by a good operator using sophisticated read-out equipment will ensure that your engine is tuned to its proper potential.

An often overlooked way of releasing an engine's potential is to ensure that its exhaust system is tuned to perfection.

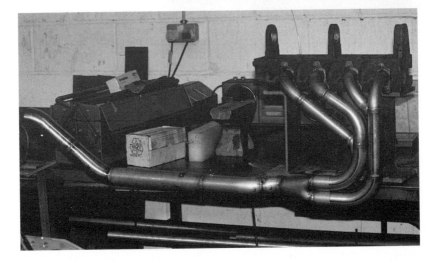

Immaculate preparation and presentation are taken for granted in professional motor racing, but they should also be the aim for the club amateur.

What a miserable contrast this picture offers; the scrutineer would be thoroughly unimpressed by the sight of so much gunge.

Welding kit seems to be synonymous with motorsport, but be sure that whoever uses it is fully conversant with the safety rules; there are several good books on the subject on the market.

One day you may need a tow, so a strong hook clearly visible beneath the front valance is a sensible precaution because it could save you vital seconds getting back to the paddock.

Roll-cages take many forms and only the best should be the rule. Also, I think I would be insisting on rather more padding if I were racing this car.

An example of a cage doing its job. The rolled Porsche may look sad, but its driver emerged unscathed.

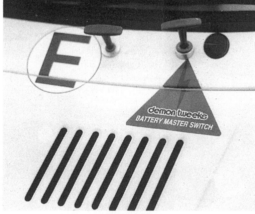

One of the most
important items of car
preparation – a neatly
plumbed-in mechanical
fire extinguishing system
securely bolted to the
floor of the car.

Both the extinguisher and
the mandatory battery
master switches should
be clearly identified on
the outside of the
bodywork.

A wind-cheating but
equally effective solution
recessed into the
bodywork of an Aston
Martin.

Drilled aluminium plates attached to the pedal pads and carefully positioned to achieve maximum driver comfort and pedal control. Note also the invaluable footrest to the left of the clutch pedal.

Door netting may look unsightly, but it offers useful impact protection, particularly if competing with the door window lowered.

A clean and unfussy instrument and control panel, with the dials angled towards the driver. Ideally, the extinguisher pull-handle should be clearly marked.

A tachometer with the telltale reading a touch over 7,000rpm. It is sensible to angle the dial so that the engine's optimum rpm is at the top.

Good car control starts with fitting a robust, comfortable and safely engineered steering wheel.

Ballast, whether required to increase weight or improve balance, should always be bolted securely to the floorpan.

Tracking the wheels is as important at the rear of the car as it is at the front.

Production cars usually have to compete at a minimum homologated weight, which can cause the occasional anxious moment in the scrutineering bay.

Tyre choice will always be an important factor in car performance. On the left is a 185x55-13 and on the right a 185x60-13, the latter's tread having been buffed to a 4mm depth to produce a squarer tread.

A set of front and rear wet-weather tyres sharing a rack with a solid-tread slick. Changing weather conditions are a perpetual nightmare for the racing driver.

Your first task on arriving at a circuit and taking up your allotted parking space in the paddock is to sign on, remembering to bring your Competition Licence with you.

In the scrutineering bay the emphasis will be on every aspect of safety and, increasingly these days, noise pollution.

Ticket to race. The 'Passed by Scrutineer' sticker should be displayed prominently, an ideal place on a saloon being the side window behind the driver.

A time for your undivided attention. The driver's briefing prior to racing is both mandatory and the time when crucial last-minute instructions or advice are offered by the Clerk of the Course.

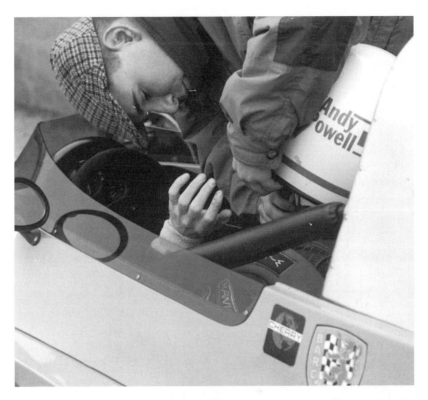

In the tense moments
leading up to the start
details like helmet
adjustment can often
benefit from a spot of
outside assistance; be
sure that one of your
crew is on hand.

Never skimp on the
quality of your footware,
and be sure that your
shoes are tight but not
over-tight. Also, in wet
weather the soles should
be wiped dry as you
climb aboard.

Despite practising all the best lines, once the racing starts you have to make best use of the track space available and seize opportunities as they are offered.

This is what it is all about. The thrill of acknowledging the chequered flag as you cross the finishing line; if yours is the first car across so much the better, and if not – well, there's always the next time.

CHAPTER 5

Further preparation

"In motor racing there is no substitute for horsepower."
Anon

Much has been expressed in recent years concerning the unfair advantage afforded to some drivers by the superiority of their equipment. The corollary to this is that the driver is of less importance than the technology and – taking this line of thinking to the extreme – becomes largely redundant. The idea that this view is a strictly contemporary one, however, is misleading, because the attribution of a particular car's success to its superiority has been around for a long time. Each individual improvement in technology on the track has been initiated by the desire to win, and the arguments that rage today about the use of fly-by-wire technology and aids like traction control are only a repetition of the furore way back that accompanied the move from front to rear-engined Formula One cars and the numerous innovations caused by materials development over the years from specialist alloys to Kevlar. Perhaps eventually it will become necessary for ruling bodies only to allow the inclusion of technological advances that improve safety rather than just performance.

On a smaller scale, but still of major importance to the competitors involved, are the disputes that occur at club events as to whether a particular car is complying with the relevant technical regulations. This is particularly prevalent in one-make series where any small, and possibly illegal, tweak can mean the difference of a fraction of a second per lap – which can sometimes be enough to provide the recipient with an unbeatable advantage.

In most non-team sports, personal ability can be compared on an equal basis in terms of skill, strength or stamina, and it is easy, for instance, to measure the performance of a boxer or an athlete by the number of fights or races he has won. In motorsport, however, the abilities of a competitor can be less apparent if the car in question is not as well-developed or has been less carefully prepared than others, and in these circumstances it is often quite difficult for true talent to shine through. Therefore, you should strive to always come to the line in a car that will be both fast and reliable as a result of the attention to detail and high build quality that has been put into its preparation; that way, you may well have already gained the edge over drivers of equal ability.

This chapter, therefore, is concerned with improving the car beyond the basic requirements of safety regulations, which, because of their importance, will almost certainly have dominated your initial preparation work – after all, if the car is not safe, there is no way that will even be allowed to compete.

Weight
When British Airways made the decision to switch from

lead crystal to cut glass for the drinks they provide for their First Class passengers on long-haul flights, they were not aiming just to reduce the capital cost involved. Instead, the move was part of a concerted campaign aimed at incrementally reducing the all-up weight of their aircraft, so that less fuel could be used for each flight. You may think that such initiatives are insignificant in relation to the overall costs of running a major airline, but each tiny loss in weight had a useful cumulative effect and caused measurable savings over a period of time.

This same technique can be used to good effect when you consider improving the performance of your race car as in most instances the less weight it carries, the faster it will travel. When you look closely at a supposedly stripped-out saloon car you will often find that it still has unnecessary items such as heaters and carpets that can also be removed, and there are other less obvious ways in which the weight can be reduced significantly. Much of what you can do will be determined by the series regulations, which need to be examined closely, but here are a few examples:

• Excess internal trim such as door and rear-side panelling. However, note that you will need to sheet over the door shell, preferably in aluminium.

• Rear wash/wiper and motor, if fitted.

• Sound-deadening pads that are factory-applied to larger body panels to prevent drumming.

• Glovebox, door pockets, heater controls and vents.

• Headlining. I am surprised that the *Blue Book* does not require it to be removed for safety reasons anyway as in a fire it could melt or ignite.

• Mudflaps, unless you are rallying the car, when heavy-duty types would be required.

• External trim such as side rubbing strips.

• Extraneous nuts and bolts, brackets and clips no longer needed.

• Underseal for whilst it may not seem worth bothering with the task of stripping the car's underside of its underseal, this can weigh a considerable amount.

The ideal, albeit expensive, solution to the weight problem, and one practised by works teams, is to start off with a bare shell that can be modified to suit your own requirements. If it is taken off the production line at an early stage of its build, it is likely to still be in bare metal – race cars do not need the excess weight of layers of paint – and with none of the various fittings and brackets that the final version carries. This has additional benefits, aside from minimizing weight, in that a bare shell is easier to work on, being unencumbered by seats, facia and windows. Seam welding, for instance, as described earlier, is a far simpler task, as is paint-spraying the inside of the car.

In order to ensure that cars compete on an equal basis, all one-make series specify a minimum weight for the car concerned. This usually allows a reasonable deduction from the production version's original kerb weight for items that are not needed, but if you were to undertake all of the weight-saving measures listed above it is likely that the car would be too light. If you are limited to a minimum weight, an advantage can be gained by redistributing the weight to where it best benefits the handling of the car which, logically, is the lowest point in order to decrease the centre of gravity. So, if you are tight on your minimum weight requirement it follows that the areas that you should concentrate on lightening most are those that are above floor level.

This same principle should be used when you install anything new on the car such as your race seat, or if the regulations allow you to move the battery position, for example. In addition to the benefit of not having the battery situated in a vulnerable position under the bonnet or in the boot, repositioning it in a sealed box in the passenger footwell also helps in a small way to lower the car's centre of gravity.

Where a minimum weight is not specified, or the requirement is less onerous, there are considerable advantages to be gained by taking quite major steps to lighten the car. These can include replacing body panels with glassfibre or composite plastic alternatives, fitting Perspex windows and examining each component in minute detail to lessen its weight or replacing it with a lighter alternative.

In all instances, however, you should be careful not to take this exercise to such extremes that you jeopardize the structural integrity of the car or adversely affect the reliability of any of its components. Whilst on this subject, it is worth remembering my earlier comment that if you replace the original steel driver's door with a glassfibre shell, you are obliged to fit side bars within the rollcage to protect you from a side impact. That said, it is worth fitting them, even if the door has not been lightened, both for safety reasons and to increase rollcage rigidity.

If you cannot replace panels with lighter alternatives, another time-honoured method of reducing weight is to drill holes or cut out excess metal in non-structural bodywork. As one can imagine, this should not be attempted by the inexperienced as it could jeopardize the overall strength of the car when subjected to racing stresses or in the event of a collision. Nevertheless, the cumulative weight loss can be worthwhile if the job is well-executed and enthusiasm with the drill and angle grinder is tempered by caution.

To conclude, it is worth briefly mentioning the subject of ballast. This is used to equalize cars of different performance, as in the BTCC where rear-wheel-drive cars are obliged to carry extra weight, or to equalize individual drivers according to their success, as in the Renault 5TS Championship, where the winner of a race has to carry a weight penalty in the next round.

Suspension

It is easy to assume from the opening quotation that the engine alone is the key to power, and therefore to competing effectively and winning. However, if you have ever taken a road car, even a high-performance one, onto a circuit you will have soon realized that the constraining factor on your speed is not a lack of power, but poor handling. Even the most powerful and exotic road cars, with a few notable exceptions, have been designed to balance the need for performance with that of comfort and a smooth ride. This is because despite their sporting pretensions most of these cars will spend their lives having to endure the same potholes, kerbs and undulating road surfaces as more humdrum machinery, so their suspension designs must be a compromise – the opposite, in fact, to the majority of off-road leisure pursuit vehicles in that they will probably have to climb nothing more extreme than the kerb outside the cashpoint machine in the High Street.

Such concern for comfort is not a consideration in a race car, however, where performance takes precedence over all other factors and a harsh ride is just a part of the price to be paid.

Notwithstanding the simple fact that improving the handling will enable a car to lap a circuit quicker, when compared pound for pound with the cost of installing a more powerful engine it makes sound economic sense as well.

As you can imagine, there are many different types of suspension, and each model of car will have been the subject of a separate design. That said, a number of principles are common to all systems and it is important to familiarize yourself with the suspension type and layout of your own car and have a clear understanding of the function of all the key components – in other words, how it all works. There are many training and technical books on suspension design which offer a basic insight of the subject, while the official workshop manual for your own car should provide you with the necessary details of its particular layout and its set-up.

The prospect of upgrading and optimizing your suspension can be fairly daunting because even after some research into the subject you are likely to be entering uncharted territory as you discover that any adjustment to one element leads to another being altered elsewhere. It is therefore advisable for the novice to use the services of a specialist experienced in setting up suspensions who will have all the equipment necessary for carrying out the required checks and adjustments.

Bear in mind, though, that having such a company perform mundane tasks like renewing bushes is an expensive option, so some form of compromise will inevitably be needed, such as perhaps getting them to provide you with an assessment of your existing set-up together with recommendations.

For many of the popular saloon cars being raced there are settings that have been tried and tested. So, to save a lot of time and effort it is worth undertaking as much research as you can to discover them. The following list of suggestions should at least point you in the right direction:
• Speak in turn to the Technical Scrutineer, Chairman and Secretary for the particular race series. Please note, however, that this does not mean interrogating them in turn, but rather making a polite request for advice as a newcomer.
• Similarly, attend meetings and speak to fellow competitors. Within reason it should also be possible to take a look at what they have already done on their cars (but please remember to ask first, especially if you want to take a

photograph for future reference!). You will often learn more in a few minutes from someone who is prepared to share information that is already common knowledge in the paddock than through many seasons of trial and error on your own.

• If you are preparing a car of a model that has already been raced substantially, it is worthwhile asking the advice of someone who has raced one previously. This is particularly valid if the car has moved to a different class or race series over the years through a larger engine or a facelift. Much of the development work undertaken on early cars is usually readily transferable and still valid.

• Visit or telephone a race parts company that specializes in your particular model and ask their advice as to parts availability and prices. There are also a great number of race-car preparation and tuning companies that may be able to help you.

• Consult any published material on modifying your car. Books dedicated to one particular model tend to be for the most popular cars, but do not overlook car magazines, especially the back issues, and the owners clubs if applicable.

Finally, when you have accumulated all of this, sometimes conflicting, advice it is time to put it into practice. Whether you are undertaking the work yourself or having it done for you, the starting point will always be to examine the car's current set-up so that you can improve and modify from a known base position. As one can imagine, the complexities of suspension tuning cannot be explored in detail, but you should look at each of the main settings, how they can be measured and the effect of altering them. Some useful titles dedicated specifically to the subject of suspension are contained in the recommended reading list at the back of the book.

If you are serious about your racing, no matter the level at which you are competing, it is highly desirable that you know as much as possible about suspension geometry and its effect on a car's handling characteristics. It is not helpful when testing your car on a track to encounter a handling problem and be reduced to simply saying to someone from whom you are seeking a cure: "It feels a bit wobbly," or: "It's like driving a fridge." The use of the correct and widely-used terminology will help you to communicate the problem effectively and prevent potentially embarrassing silences.

Corner weights
In addition to the measures already outlined to reduce the overall weight of the car, it is also necessary to ensure that as far as possible there is an even distribution of weight between each corner of the car (in other words, by each wheel). This, in theory, should mean that the car will be evenly balanced, exhibit predictable handling characteristics insofar as it will behave in the same manner when travelling around a left-hand as a right-hand bend and should also be more stable in a straight line. This tends to overlook the effect of weight transference that occurs during braking, accelerating and cornering, but at least the car, if it is evenly balanced at rest, will be more controllable when at speed because of its consistent behaviour.

To measure the corner weights accurately, it is best to set the car up on four individual electronic scales made specifically for this purpose so that any local adjustment can be assessed overall. For the club racer on a limited budget, however, it is possible to obtain results, albeit more slowly, with the aid of a simple mechanical weight gauge.

If the car is especially light it is even possible to use a set of bathroom scales and three blocks of wood of the same height as the scales at rest. One word of warning, though: this cannot be done if the car is too heavy, and a rule of thumb is that the scales should be able to take a minimum load equal to 30 per cent of the total weight of the car. This makes it ideal for setting up single-seaters and small light saloon cars, therefore, but it is impractical for anything heavier. If using this system, the corner weights are adjusted quite simply – in theory, anyway – by raising or lowering the height of each corner or, in other words, the amount of weight which is bearing down through the suspension.

First, with the car on a flat and even surface, jack up each corner and place the blocks under three of the wheels, positioning the scales beneath the fourth wheel, but leaving the jack in place. Then, after gently rocking the car to release any parts of the suspension that may be binding, and with the driver seated in the car to reflect actual conditions, carefully lower the jack until the car is fully supported on each wheel, then make a note of the reading on the scales. When this has been completed for each corner by swapping over the scales with a block in turn, you should have the weight being exerted at each wheel. For this reason it does not matter if the recorded weights are slightly inaccurate as all you are doing is making an empirical comparison. The weight recorded at each corner is likely to be different, depending on the car's natural weight bias, engine position and existing suspension set-up. But as a rule of thumb you should be aiming for an even weight distribution between one side of the car and the other, with the bias front-to-rear dependent on whether you are driving the front or rear wheels.

In a rear-wheel-drive car it is best to try to get as much weight as far back as possible, not only to help traction, but because during braking any weight will be exerted toward the front of the car, which in turn will lighten the rear and make oversteer more likely. In a front-wheel-drive car the same need for weight over the driving wheels exists. As an aside, it is this reduction of weight at the back of the car that provokes the common phenomenon of the rear brakes locking up and causing the car to become unstable: the less weight acting on a brake, the less resistance there is to it locking up.

Adjustment of corner weights is dependant on the type of suspension, but basically it involves lengthening or shortening the suspension height at each corner individually until the desired weight is achieved on the scales under the loaded wheel. Practically, this means fitting new longer or shorter springs or packing them out, and whilst simple in theory, this can become a matter of repetitive adjustments and checks as any change to one corner has a resultant effect on the others. When complete, however, the correct setting-up of the corner weights is certainly a job well done.

Camber

Camber, the inward or outward tilt of a wheel from upright, plays an important part in determining the effective area of tyre surfaces in contact with the track during cornering at speed. With most tyres being at their most effective when square to the track, it is necessary to anticipate the amount of positive camber induced by bodyroll and to build a static amount of negative camber into the suspension to offset this so that, during cornering, the camber is zero. Too much negative camber, however, is just as bad as too little, and in some cases even positive camber will be beneficial. In a car experiencing severe understeer, positive camber to the rear wheels will allow the back end to slide and step out more. It is not the total solution, and you must also look at such aspects as bodyroll and spring stiffness, but as a first step it is worth trying.

To find out how your car is handling it is worth photographing or, better still, videoing it as it enters and travels around a corner, although the ideal situation is to use on-board telemetry. For club racing, though, a combination of accepted good practice and the trained eye of an experienced observer will usually be sufficient. The majority of road cars have fixed camber, but most lower arms can be fitted with offset bushes or substituted with longer variants to alter the settings. Wherever possible you should fit fully adjustable lower arms, which you can then vary with accuracy.

Toe-in/toe-out

Road cars require a degree of toe-in to ensure straight-line stability whereas a car on a race track must instead be set up correctly for cornering. As it is necessary to evaluate each car according to other prevailing criteria, generalizations at this stage would be dangerous, but suffice to say that even minor adjustments will have a marked effect on handling.

Full adjustment is not often possible in a production road car transferred to the track, but this should not dissuade you from having a full check on the existing settings, which at least will provide you with base information from which to work. The development of more sophisticated equipment has led to a growth in four-wheel alignment and adjustment specialists who will be able to help you.

Uprating components

When trying to alter the car's suspension settings you will also benefit greatly by replacing many of the standard components with uprated versions as, aside from them being stronger and engineered for the specific task of racing, many – as mentioned earlier – are also adjustable and can be altered to suit your requirements. Again, you will largely be constrained by the technical regulations as to what you may replace, and much will depend on your car's individual characteristics, but typical areas for close examination include:

Bushes The standard rubber bushes on a road car are a compromise between rigidity for a positive feel and flexibility to ensure comfort through less noise transmission, with the latter usually winning. Simply replacing all of the old and perished rubber bushes on your car will transform it immediately, but for the best results less yielding materials need to be used. Generally, there are two options: the first and easiest is to use Nylatron or a self-lubricating polythene that is far more rigid than rubber, but will nevertheless not 'bind'; the second, better, option is to fit Rose joints. These are metal-to-metal connections that remove the problem of flexing entirely, but require careful and periodic inspection for wear.

Anti-roll bars Uprated (thicker) anti-roll bars at both the front and rear of a car will have a marked effect on limiting the amount of bodyroll through corners, although in some cases, when too stiff, they can lead to the handling being adversely affected, especially in the wet. It may appeal in theory to have a set-up rather like a go-kart, but in reality this will make the car too rigid, cause excess understeer and make any point of instability less predictable. With a kart you can steer on the throttle and to a small degree shift your weight on corners, but in a larger and heavier vehicle this is not possible and it will behave very abruptly. On the track this will manifest itself when cornering with the back end of the car suddenly spinning out without prior and graduated warning.

Fitting adjustable anti-roll bars is therefore a useful solution as the stiffness can be altered to suit the individual's preference, depending on the circuit and the prevailing conditions.

Springs and dampers Aside from their effect on ride height and corner weights, springs have a critical role to play in determining the frequency and amplitude of any suspension bounce. This is caused by the inherent material characteristics of the spring and, in particular, the spring rate, which will determine how the car reacts through a corner or is able to cope with vertical movement caused by track undulations, crests and bumps.

Dampers effectively control the amount of sprung movement, and uprated versions are a worthwhile fitting as inadequate damping will allow the car to dive under braking, squat under acceleration in FWD cars, and generally bounce unchecked when cornering (the classic hopping syndrome). Fitting uprated dampers will also have a marked effect on braking, ensuring the wheels are not allowed to flutter rapidly over the track surface, thereby reducing grip, due to unchecked spring oscillation. Whenever adjustable dampers are fitted, ensure that these are first set to their mid-range position to enable a base to be established from which to work.

Tyres

If you consider that when racing you will be relying at best on the equivalent of two square feet of rubber to be in contact with the surface of the track, this is clearly an area of the car that demands close attention to maximize performance.

As with suspension, the whole issue of tyre technology could fill an entire book on its own and is an interesting area for further research. In the limited space available, however, I have tried to cover the basic principles and describe the ways in which tyres can be used to your advantage.

The great number of tyre manufacturers eager for your business means that you are faced with a bewildering array from which to choose, so selection by popular and fashionable brand name is perhaps not the best starting point. What you need to do first is establish a size, then a specification for the type of tyre you will need, based on performance, longevity and cost. All tyres have a combination of the best and worst attributes of these factors and it is up to you to decide which is more important.

Starting with the size of tyre, this may already be specified in the class regulations; in some one-make series there is actually a 'control' tyre, provided at a discounted price by a single manufacturer, which all competitors must run (plus a variant for use in the wet). This arrangement means that the tyre manufacturer has the cachet of their own series without the fear of opposition and the competitors are all equally shod, so therefore have the same performance and subsidized costs. If the series is being taken quite seriously it is not unknown for those who are devious – and rich – enough, to try to establish whether different batches of tyres have better handling properties, but I think this is taking it all a little too far. Instead, it is far better to concentrate on making sure that the tyres are buffed down to the optimum thickness of tread and are inflated to the correct pressure.

Buffing is only undertaken by a handful of tyre retailers and involves mechanically scuffing the tread on a new tyre to a lesser depth. Whilst it may appear wasteful, the buffed tyre has far better grip in the dry as the tread flexes less. Also, buffing makes tyres suffer less from overheating and the tread breaking off in chunks, thus rendering the tyre scrap in a very short space of time. The amount of tread remaining is down to individual choice and finances, with some competitors aiming to finish a race with the minimum legal tread of 1.6mm. Ideally, 4-5mm is an effective compromise, enabling the most heavily loaded tyre on the car to last for a few races before needing replacement.

If tyre size is unrestricted, you may benefit by choosing a size that has a desired effect on your gearing. In simple terms this means that the smaller the overall wheel diameter the greater the acceleration, but conversely the lower the top speed – and *vice versa*.

The aspect ratio of the tyre is an expression of the effective height of the tyre divided by the width. This gives a percentage of around 70-80 for road tyres, and as little as 35 for race tyres. Smaller aspect ratios are generally accepted as being the best in terms of improving stability, grip and steering response, but this does not always hold true if the tyre has exceptional grip because in such a situation the tyre wall may be so short and thin that it will flex and roll away under the wheel. A tyre with a slightly larger aspect ratio in the same situation may have a stiffer wall that would be more likely to resist the effect of the grip.

In all cases, if you are considering changing your overall wheel diameter by fitting a tyre with a different aspect ratio, or even a wider tyre, it is advisable to seek the advice of a tyre supplier to ensure that it is compatible with your wheel type and check that when fitted it will not foul the suspension, steering or bodywork.

Finally, as mentioned already, only trial and error will prove which are the best tyres for you to use, and whilst it may seem obvious, it is worth checking the tyres that the front runners are using.

Tyre pressures are critical whatever tyre you are running. Too low a pressure will lead to them becoming overheated and damaged whilst too high a pressure can reduce their optimum tread width. A general rule of thumb is that your race temperatures should not be causing the tyre to increase inflation by more than 10psi, but do not try to prosecute me if this does not work: all tyres are different and work better at marginally different temperatures and pressures. Again, it is all down to testing.

Brakes

"Who needs brakes? They only slow you down!" This is a frequent comment that proves, perhaps, how many drivers fail to realize the dramatic effect that good brakes can have on improving lap times. In performance terms, available braking power is almost as critical as acceleration and, like suspension modifications, it is not that expensive to upgrade them and very cheap indeed to learn how to use them to their optimum. For example, consider two cars of equal performance but one having better brakes. The car that can slow down later at a corner will have remained faster for longer and will therefore have travelled a greater distance than the other. If there are five braking points per lap and at each the time differential between the two cars is only 2/10ths of a second, it follows that the one fitted with a better braking system will cross the line at least a full 10 seconds ahead of the other after a 10-lap race. In reality, however, this speed differential will be much greater as acceleration will occur earlier and so have a greater effect. Having an excellent braking system is only of benefit, however, if you are confident as to its capabilities and know exactly where, when and how hard to use the brake pedal in order to maintain your maximum performance for lap after lap – which yet again brings us back to the need for testing, but also emphasizes the need for establishing braking points during practice.

Elaborated upon in Chapter 9, the ability to brake later and with confidence is as critical as the ability to accelerate, so following on from suspension, upgrading your braking system should be the next area for attention. Big is best, so if you have any degree of choice fit the largest brakes possible. For race series where brake systems must largely remain standard, there are still areas that can be improved quite simply and effectively, such as removing the disc stoneguards or remodelling them; fitting or increasing brake ducting; fitting uprated pads; replacing the brake system hydraulic fluid with a higher-specification racing type; and replacing rubber hoses with the braided type as this will help pedal feel.

To distribute brake forces front and rear and prevent either locking in advance of the other, a brake balance adjuster or bias can be fitted in the system. Note, however, that most regulations outlaw its ability to be used during the race, but a temporary box isolating it will overcome this. Once the optimum setting has been found in testing it is usually unnecessary to adjust it anyway unless it is a wet track.

Engines

It would be rash to try to cover the whole aspect of race engines in the short amount of space available, so instead there follows some advice on commissioning. Generally, this is the area most books conveniently omit, assuming you are either a qualified engineer or, at the other end of the scale, have unlimited funding. Most club racers are self-taught mechanics or have friends who are, and hence a combination of DIY and professional engine building will be involved. If you can afford it, your engines should always be built professionally, but if funds are stretched you should at least have the first one built properly and perhaps concentrate any burning desire you have to build one yourself to a back-up unit instead. The best method of choosing a good engine builder is by personal recommendation and through looking at results.

Rolling roads

Once you have installed a new engine it is pointless to assume that any static settings you have used are the optimum for performance. I know of someone who once spent a lot of money on having an engine built, but then entrusted it to his local accessory and garage chain to 'tune it up'. Now, I am not casting doubts on such a company's ability to do a fine change of oil and plugs, but performance engine tuning is a different matter entirely and requires sophisticated facilities and equipment.

There is no mystique to rolling roads: they are simply a way of setting up and optimizing a car under load and near-realistic conditions rather than just relying on static adjustments or the lengthy and inaccurate procedure of adjusting and then track-testing various settings. As they are empirical, they tend to give quantifiable readings and graphical measurements of performance and so are particularly useful for developing a car's engine in a practical way to its maximum potential. Good examples of this include experimenting with different inlet manifolds or exhaust systems to find the best one for your set of circumstances. It may take time, and rolling roads are not cheap in that respect, but at least you should end up with a known and quantifiable output.

Be wary of grandiose claims by engine builders and fellow competitors alike who may try to be economical with the truth about their engines: put your trust instead in the printout from a modern rolling road. This will tell you in graphic form the power at the wheels – where it matters – the transmission losses and, most important of all, where the usable power is within the rev band. Adjusting the engine settings to move the power curve to where it is more useful is much cheaper and more effective than just trying to increase the overall peak power. Also, knowing just where the most torque is being developed can be used to great effect on the track and will hopefully encourage you to keep the engine working within its optimum power range, hence the value of those 'shift lights'.

Testing

There are essentially three reasons for taking to the track in advance of a race: to test the car; to increase driver experience; and to improve circuit familiarity. Each of these separately, but preferably combined, will result in helping you to be both quicker and safer.

Car testing

In the long winter months before the club motor racing season begins, drivers and their mechanics will have devoted considerable time, money and effort to trying to squeeze every last ounce of power from their car. Many hours will have been spent combing the technical regulations to see if there any modifications that can be carried out to improve performance that may have been overlooked by fellow competitors and therefore might provide an edge.

All of this is essential if you want to be up with the front runners, but what should not be forgotten is the need for the driver to be as well-prepared as the car and be aware of its capabilities.

As touched on above, an aspect commonly overlooked is that your newly acquired/modified/improved race car is likely to be another unknown factor, and there is a clear advantage to be gained by being familiar with its handling characteristics and performance prior to the all-absorbing task of driving it in competition. Therefore, some form of pre-season testing is essential to facilitate this familiarization, to set the car up properly and to rectify any problems that may come to light.

This need not be expensive if you choose a half-day session midweek and pick a less obvious venue such as Goodwood, for instance, which is no longer used for circuit racing, but whose track is still sufficiently varied and demanding for test purposes. Whatever the cost of testing compared with your stretched budget, remember that it will always be less than the typical fees for a single meeting, so it can be considered a wise investment. Besides, it is surely better to experience the mysteries of a loose-fitting HT lead in private rather than at your first race of the season.

As has been emphasized throughout this book, preparation is essential, even prior to testing, as time is money – and usually in as limited supply. You should therefore set yourself a schedule of what you want to test in advance and make sure you take as many tools and spares as you can carry. As someone who has spent a frantic afternoon trying to locate a replacement exhaust valve which had decided to succumb to Uri Geller, take my advice and pack *everything*, no matter how unlikely, you believe, that it will be needed.

The car's suspension should already have been basically set up to known parameters and the engine optimized through a session on a rolling road prior to arrival at the track, so the first few laps should be gradual and hold no surprises. Then, after five laps, the car should be taken into the pit area for a basic check of the engine bay and to set the tyre pressures equally. It is a matter of preference as to what is adjusted first, as any incremental change to any of the components will have an effect on the way the car handles, and this perhaps is where most mistakes are made. It is imperative that all changes are single actions and noted down, or you will be unable to gauge whether it has caused an improvement. A driver may believe that the car is becoming quicker whereas the opposite may be true, so it is important to record lap times as well as just relying on judgment. For the same reason it is essential that like is compared with like. Therefore, do not be swayed by different lap times from different drivers; keep as many constants as possible and concentrate on those aspects that you change.

A good technique for establishing optimum settings is to consider the extremes and then make adjustments until a happy medium is reached, often without the detailed knowledge of the driver. An example of this is to try the tyre pressures both high and then low, making notes of lap times accordingly and varying them each time until the recorded times are at their quickest. It is also a sure way of testing the driver, who will be unaware of what you have adjusted, only its effect.

Driver testing

This is largely covered later so I will not dwell on the subject, but some form of racing tuition, even for a few hours, at your nearest circuit will pay dividends in assessing and correcting your faults and building up your confidence for the forthcoming season, even if you are an experienced driver, as everyone gets rusty.

Too often, drivers enter the sport with only minimal racetrack awareness, and whilst everyone must start as a 'rookie' there is no excuse for not having taken the time and minimal expense of elementary tuition for their own benefit and for that of others.

Circuit familiarity

No drivers, however skilled and experienced, will be able to maximize their abilities if they are unfamiliar with the circuit on which they are about to race. As covered in Chapter 7, a sensible way of obtaining a basic idea of a circuit's layout and characteristics is to take a walk around it prior to the meeting officially starting; obviously, anyone who takes the trouble to do this will be that much better prepared when the time comes to begin formal practice. Of course, wholly dedicated drivers who have both the budget and the time will doubtless have visited the venue midweek. By doing so, not only will they have been able to familiarize themselves with the circuit and consequently decrease their lap times on it, but they will also have been able to carry out any adjustments necessary to the car in order to maximize its performance. There is no such thing as too much testing.

CHAPTER 6

Safety fast

"In my sport the quick are too often listed among the dead."
Jackie Stewart
Jonathon Green, *A Dictionary of Contemporary Quotations*,
1982

"I don't mind having an accident as long as I can see it
coming."
Nigel Mansell
Sunday Telegraph, September 23, 1989

Motorsport can kill you – a rather melodramatic statement
and a negative note on which to start, but unfortunately,
each time you compete you are at risk of being involved in
an accident and you have no way of knowing just how
serious it may be. This applies just as much to hillclimbing
events as circuit racing, perhaps even more so when one
considers the absence of a permanent 'safety culture' at
some of these low-key events.

To put all this in perspective, though, fatalities and serious injuries within motorsport are, thankfully, very rare in comparison with other types of sport, particularly activities such as swimming and diving, which contain the highest risk.

Whilst the overall figures relating to fatalities and injuries may be low, much of this can be attributed to effective preventative and reactive measures being taken through the use of good equipment and by prompt action by those unsung heroes, the marshals. The safety culture in motor racing generally is exemplary, but this should not lead you into any sense of complacency; although statistically you are relatively safe when racing, everyone who competes runs the risk – however slight – of being involved in a potentially life-threatening incident at any time. Therefore, you must equip yourself for the worst possible case, which could involve both physical damage and fire.

So far, concentration has mainly centred on preparing the car to be a potential race winner whilst remaining safe, but equally important is ensuring that this same preparation and attention to detail benefits you, the driver.

Safety clothing

Nearly every book or magazine article you will read on safety clothing will tell you to buy the best – a view I share to a certain degree, but with some reservations. With race fees increasing each year and the overall cost of motorsport being so high, I am also a realist and know that many drivers, especially in their first season, will simply be unable to buy the best available equipment, which can cost a small fortune, and be more likely to spend most of their available money on ensuring that their car looks its best and goes as well as possible. As an example of the expense of protection, some helmets can cost as much as the basic price of a modest but raceable car. Therefore, I favour the view that you should buy the best you can afford, the caveat being that it meets the necessary safety standards. Continuing to use the expensive helmet as an example, it may look good in the paddock, but if all you are paying for is the latest style and exquisite stitching to the lining, would it not make more sense to spend the money instead on upgrading your extinguisher system or fitting uprated brake pipes and linings?

Before individual items are assessed in more detail it must be emphasized that all safety clothing should be tried out first before purchase, and not just because there are so many styles from which to choose. Unless you are in the fortunate position of being able to order a made-to-measure tailored race suit it makes sense to avoid buying clothing via mail order if you can possibly help it. Racewear is big business and in the international marketplace it is not surprising that terms like 'small' are meaningless. An example of this is that gloves, made predominantly in Italy, where the average hands are slight, do not necessarily accord with the sizes applied in Great Britain. Still, size is not everything....

Another consideration is that part of the process of setting safety standards is to alter them periodically, thus defining a lifespan for a particular product, otherwise known as 'built-in obsolescence'. Therefore you should always check the latest edition of the *Blue Book* to verify the current relevant British or European Standards before making any purchase. Then remember that your aim is to buy clothing of the best affordable quality, which is not necessarily the most expensive, in order to protect your wallet as well as, at worst, your life.

Flame-resistant overalls

These are required to be worn by all competitors taking part in all circuit racing, sprints, hillclimbs, autocross, rallycross, drag racing and special stage rallies – in fact for all events in which wearing a helmet is compulsory. At the time of writing, overalls may be manufactured from Nomex III or Proban-treated materials as long as they comply with BS6249 Part 1 Index A or B, or are to FIA standards. In all cases you are advised to check the specification on the label carefully before you buy as there may still be old stock being sold that was manufactured prior to new standards being introduced. You should therefore be wary of large discounts being offered.

Buying a set of overalls is no different in many respects from buying a suit, although potentially more expensive and with less wear. You should always try them on in the shop for size and resist the urge to buy one that is figure-hugging, no matter how dashing you may appear. Remember that you will be wearing undergarments and that you will also need to be fairly mobile. With this in mind it is best to sit down – in the changing rooms if you are shy – and, with arms stretched out in front as if you are steering, assess whether there is enough 'give' specifically at the shoulders and under the arms and knees. If the cuffs to the arms or legs ride up, try on a larger size.

Generally, the key to resisting heat in a race suit is to have as many layers of fabric as possible as each layer traps air which acts additionally and valuably as an insulant. Even for basic motorsport a two or three-layer suit is preferable.

The all-white, box-quilted affair you saw initially in the glossy brochure may still look good in the mirror, but is totally impractical – so forget it. Instead, try to pick as dark a colour as possible, one that will not show up too much grease and dirt, preferably with some of your sponsor's main colours if you have one, or otherwise perhaps co-ordinated with the car's livery. Many of the leading race clothing manufacturers now offer a bespoke service and can design and add sponsorship lettering and logos to your racesuit depending on your budget (and that of the sponsor).

As an aside, it may be better to avoid buying orange overalls if you wish to avoid the following situation: at Snetterton, after driving up to my axles in the gravel trap at Russell's, I walked back to the car after the race, just as the tow truck arrived and began to attach a hawser to the rear tow point. As the car began to pull free I asked one of the marshals whether I should drive the car back to the pits or be towed. "Better wait for the driver," he said, "...they can be a bit touchy about us driving their cars"!

With overalls newly purchased, you can then choose suitable cloth patches, which can be stitched on, ideally with flameproof thread, in strategic places such as the upper chest and throat: these are the only parts properly visible when you are seated in the car and are therefore the most prominent areas for siting sponsors' advertising. A patch that is advisable for all racing disciplines is one bearing your name and blood group, which may seem rather gruesome at first but makes sense, as in an emergency you may be unable to give this information. Check with the shop before you leave as they may offer a personalized embroidery service or be able to put you in contact with someone locally who does.

Finally, a word of caution about cleaning your race overalls as harsh detergents can wash out the flame-retardant chemicals applied to the fabric. Read the cleaning instructions on the label, which generally will advise washing them by hand, using a weak soap solution, and as infrequently as possible. This is a good reason for keeping them clean at the circuit, which is best achieved by changing into them as late as possible and changing out of them immediately afterwards, even during the short period between practice and the race. They may be great for posing in the paddock, but they cost far too much to be used when you are working on the car.

Undergarments

Although the thought of wearing them may appear unflattering, fire-resistant underclothing is essential to protect you from the potential heat of an on-board fire which can quickly engulf a car. With temperatures exceeding 2,000deg F being recorded in typical under-bonnet fires, you are unable to rely on your racing overalls alone to protect you, so any thoughts of them being 'cissy' should be dispelled.

Long John-type leggings and vests are available in both Nomex and Proban materials, the latter being preferred by many as it tends not to itch as much (a tip is to try a liberal application of talcum powder). As with the overalls, check that the cuffs cover the ankles adequately and, similarly, that vests cover the wrist and neck areas well – the roll-neck types are ideal.

Balaclavas are available with eye holes or, particularly for those of you who wear spectacles, with a single opening. When you put it on make sure it is pulled down so that it can be tucked into the vest neckband to ensure complete coverage. Socks are easily overlooked, but are a necessary item of clothing to ensure that your feet are well protected from the risk of being burnt in a fire. Therefore, select a calf-length pair to provide adequate cover beyond your ankles and shins.

Whatever styles you choose, it is essential that they are big enough – again not just because mobility is important, but also because the trapped air in between a number of loose layers of clothing will provide a far better insulant against fire.

Finally, as in the previous section on overalls, you should be careful to follow the washing instructions for all of your undergarments in order not to render them useless.

Helmet

Crash helmets have been compulsory in motor racing since 1948, prior to which most racers relied instead on the dubious protection offered by a rearward-facing flat cap or a leather flying helmet. All helmets used for each of the racing disciplines should be made to an exacting standard, and the *Blue Book* is fairly explicit as to those that are considered acceptable. Part of the approval procedure is that suitable helmets have to bear a fluorescent yellow RAC sticker – which may already have been fixed on by the manufacturer – but if your helmet complies and does not have the sticker, it can be supplied by a scrutineer the first time it is presented, for which a nominal charge is made.

Despite the variety of shapes and styles – and range of prices – there are only two types of helmet: open and closed. The open helmet appears to have gone out of fashion in recent years – which is about the worst reason of all for selecting one type as opposed to another. Its advantages are that it does not constrict your face and so allows you to breathe easily, speak clearly and feel generally cooler. On the other hand, it does not offer much protection against flying glass and debris in a collision. Closed helmets do offer better protection to your face, especially the chin area, but as you will be strapped in firmly, this is an unlikely area of risk. In the end it is a matter of personal preference. It would be more practical for me to wear an open helmet as I would not suffer from having my spectacles steam up as much, but overall the closed helmet makes me feel more secure. If you, too, wear spectacles, it is likely that they will steam up at least for the first few minutes, so it is best to put your helmet on early to allow for this, whatever style you have chosen.

Amongst the most important items you should check are the various certification stickers which will indicate which standard the helmet meets. Two testing organizations are accepted for motorsport purposes: The British Standards Institute (helmets that comply with BS6658 – 85 Type 'A' only and BS6658 Type A/FR for FIA events), and The Snell Memorial Foundation (Snell SA 85, SA90, M85, M90). Founded in 1957 following the untimely death of William 'Pete' Snell whilst racing, the Snell Foundation are a non-profit organization dedicated to preventing head injuries or fatalities in recreational and competitive sports. This involves them undertaking comprehensive and rigorous testing of all types of helmets, from bicycle and equestrian types to crash helmets for motorsport. So, if you buy a helmet bearing one of their certifying marks you can be assured that it is fit for the purpose.

When purchasing, try on the helmet for size and, in particular, with the chin-strap tightened, pull the helmet forwards and down to check for fit. If it comes off or appears to be loose try a smaller size. Ideally, it should be snug, but not overly tight, as if it is worn for any length of time it can easily become uncomfortable. If you do not own a motorcycle it is likely that wearing a helmet will feel strange and heavy at first, and you will soon appreciate why professional drivers have such large neck muscles. With this in mind, one other accessory you may wish to consider is a neck brace, which is a horseshoe-shaped ring designed to limit and absorb the force of a jolted heavy helmet from acting on the neck muscles in an accident. Lastly, check the chin-strap mechanism as there are different types and you want one that is easy to operate and does not chafe or pinch.

Visors are not often worn in a closed car, despite the added protection they afford should the windscreen shatter or there be an intense fire. If you wish, though, it can be easily removed from your helmet and stored safely unless you wish to use the top part to carry a sponsorship message or logo. In a single-seater or open-topped car they are mandatory, however, unless goggles are worn, and are used to deflect airflow and allow you to see unimpaired. If you are not protected by a full windscreen and your helmet is in the full airstream, clear electrostatic strips can be fitted to the visor which can then be torn off periodically, along with the oil and dust that will have accumulated on them.

A tip from motorcycle applications is to treat the visor with an application of Rainex, or other similar product, that seals the tiny surface imperfections and so helps to shed water. The visor mists easily as you exhale so it is best to prevent it from closing entirely by means of a small wedge of tape or foam rubber to help air circulate more freely and using an anti-fogging gel. Finally, tinted visors are available. However, on all but the clearest of days it is probably best to avoid them as they can impair your vision. It is important to be able to see distance and detail when racing, so why not fit a sun-strip to the windscreen instead?

Obvious though it may seem, you should always take great care with your helmet and store it in a proper helmet bag whenever it is not being used so as to protect it from being scratched. In Formula One, the care of helmets is considered to be so important by drivers, who each have their helmet tailored to suit their particular requirements, that they are looked after by a specialist company at each event. Such care, albeit on a different scale, is still important at your level. As the helmet is particularly vulnerable to and from the paddock, you may wish to consider the fitting of a foam helmet carrier inside the car which will keep it secure, and always remember to use that helmet bag.

Clean the helmet regularly with a weak soap-and-water solution, not only to keep it looking good, but also because this is the best way of examining the surface of the helmet for any cracks, scratches or indentations which could easily render it weaker in the event of an accident. Consequently, it should not be modified in any way except in accordance with the manufacturer's instructions if, for instance, you are installing an intercom system. If you are considering this it is best to buy a helmet with an integral intercom system from the outset.

Should you want to make your helmet more decorative, to match the livery of the car or perhaps to display your name, it can be painted in an endless variety of colours and styles. However, this is a job that should ideally be undertaken by a specialist, as only certain paints and fixatives can be used. Normal enamel or oil-based paint, some adhesives and most cleaning agents can rearrange the molecular structure of the plastic, causing the helmet to crack or shatter under impact. As can be imagined, scrutineers are particularly stringent with helmets and will not hesitate to impound any they believe to be sub-standard, either through obvious damage or having a dull/crazed finish.

In the unfortunate event of an accident, part of the procedure involves your helmet being taken away for a visual examination by course officials, who can then impound it should they believe it to have been damaged by any impact; it is in your best interests anyway to have it checked if it has had a knock.

Gloves and boots

Most drivers, perhaps in one of their more poetic moments, will tell you that the car occasionally appears to be an extension of their own body and, if it is handling well, will describe how the car 'feels right'. One of the main contributory factors to this is probably their choice of gloves and footwear as feedback from the car is certainly enhanced by being able to handle the wheel and control the pedals with a greater degree of sensitivity.

Starting with gloves, these are compulsory for circuit racing, but are also recommended for all types of motorsport. In the event of a fire your hands are probably the area most at risk from injury as they are likely to be in contact with hot metal and plastics as well as actual flames. You should therefore choose long gauntlet-type gloves of three-ply Nomex that are thick whilst also being pliable enough to allow movement. As a guide, when trying on your gloves you should be able to flex your fingers easily, but note that as most gloves tend to stretch slightly with wear do not pick a size that is more in keeping with gardening. Aside from the safety benefits, a well-fitting pair of gloves will also prevent your hands, which perhaps will be sweating a little, from slipping on the wheel and consequently will give you a more positive grip.

Because of the expense that has to be borne when starting out, boots are often considered as some form of luxury, but from a practical point of view they help to give a better feel for the pedals as they have a thinner sole. As the heel is bevelled, they make it easier to operate the pedals and, being non-slip, they enable you to feel more sure of your foot movements, which tend to be more precise. Safety-wise they are generally all-leather in order to resist heat well, and they extend quite high up the ankle to offer additional protection. It is very tempting, but do not wear training shoes as these can melt and are not made for the job, despite the high cost of some makes. That said, you may be able to manage for a while with all-leather training shoes, but will undoubtedly notice a considerable difference once you try some specialist racing boots.

Before leaving the issue of safety clothing it is worth mentioning that to keep it all together, clean and safe you should make use of a large kitbag which should be checked through before you leave home. Until a few years back it was possible to leave all manner of tools, equipment and kit unattended at circuits, but more recently the number of items that mysteriously 'take a walk' has increased, though thankfully this tendency is less noticeable at single club events. It is therefore prudent to keep your kitbag out of sight in the boot, and away from temptation.

Circuit safety

Racing is dynamic and demands split-second decisions and action, not only to compete effectively, but also to respond in an emergency: your safety on the track is affected as much by acting appropriately as being adequately clothed. Being prepared for all eventualities is difficult, but the care and attention you spend in making sure the car is safe will help you to diagnose any problems and be in a better position to know what action to take when something goes wrong. Examples of this include ensuring that the remote electrical isolator and fire extinguisher pull-handle are within reach, or simply being so familiar with the harness buckle operation that you can release it and get out of the car as second nature – very useful if you are upside down at the time. Similarly, the effort you have made to become competent as a driver will complement the reliability and safety of the car and certainly narrow the odds of anything untoward happening. If it does, you should be in a better position to determine what needs to be done.

Flags

Flags play an important role in being the only practicable way of communicating information from the course officials to the drivers virtually instantaneously, although the value of this prompt action often goes unrecognized. Each of the flags and the manner in which they are shown have a different meaning, warning the driver of a current or imminent situation, and so should not go unheeded. However, this is easier said than done, and in the heat of the race strict and immediate observance of flags requires a high degree of discipline on the part of the driver. Much of the problem lies in drivers not being aware of the flags being waved, which I can believe, not because the flags are so small, but simply because drivers are preoccupied with racing and so not looking for them. Also, many drivers seem to be completely unaware of where the marshals posts are sited on the circuit. This latter situation is unforgivable, because it shows a disregard not only for their own safety, but also that of other drivers and the marshals themselves. As frequently advocated elsewhere, walking around the track early in the day will enable these posts to be identified, and they must later be verified, from the driving seat, during the practice session and on the assembly lap.

Dealing with each of the flag signals in turn, it can be seen that although they provide specific information it is only in a general context, so vigilance and preparedness are essential. For example, a waved yellow flag signals danger, indicative perhaps of a car that has spun off the circuit, or a multiple crash that is about to block the complete track ahead of you, so your actions should anticipate the worst possible situation.

National flag
This is occasionally used instead of the green and red lights, particularly for starting those cars at the back of the grid that have a 10-second penalty. It is also used to start the second half of a split grid.

Blue flag
Held aloft, but stationary, this indicates that another faster car – or cars – is (are) approaching. Your actions in this instance should be to identify the car(s) concerned and in the small amount of time available determine which way their drivers are likely to overtake. Much at this point will depend on your relative positions on the track and the orientation of the next corner. If it is obvious that the following car can pass you more easily on one side than the other, then signal to them using the appropriate hand, check

that they are aware of your intentions and move over to give them sufficient room to pass. This courtesy is not only polite, but much safer, especially if the overtaking car is passing you at a considerable speed. All of the manoeuvres described should be fluid and gradual as any sudden movements could lead to a misunderstanding between drivers, a loss of control, or your car being off-line for the approaching corner.

If the blue flag is waved, this indicates that another driver is actually trying to overtake, of which you should already be aware through regular checks in your mirrors; it is essential that you are conscious of your position relative to other cars and drivers on a continual basis. Should a faster car approach you undetected and you are flagged, again do not make any sudden moves – the onus to overtake safely is on the faster driver, who is quite aware of where you are.

White flag
Held stationary, this flag indicates that a service vehicle or slow-moving race car is on the circuit ahead of you; when waved, it means that this is occurring close by, so beware. A slower-moving vehicle is usually easy to spot – providing, of course, it is in your line of vision – but you may be going around a blind bend or a tight hairpin. Wherever the particular vehicle is, the fact that it is on the track should alert you to the possibility of an incident ahead, so be prepared for that situation as well as actually coming upon the vehicle itself.

Yellow flag
Held stationary, the yellow flag means 'Danger, slow down sufficiently to ensure that full control of the vehicle can be retained. No overtaking'. If the flag is waved it means 'Great danger. Slow down considerably. Be prepared to change suddenly from the projected racing line, or take

other evasive action, including stopping if necessary. No overtaking'.

These quotations, direct from the *Blue Book*, are explicit. Nevertheless, the yellow flag still causes great difficulty to competitors who either do not see it, choose not to slow down, or continue to overtake. Often, to compound the problem, if one competitor sees the flag and slows down, another – less observant – driver may then overtake as a result. This is not an action that can be condoned, but in some circumstances I can have a certain amount of sympathy with the second driver if subsequently he is called before the Clerk of the Course. However, there is ultimately no excuse for ignoring a yellow flag – only, perhaps, extenuating circumstances that the Clerk of the Course may or may not take into account. Knowing this should make you even more vigilant.

Words such as 'sufficiently' and 'considerably' are indicative, but vague, as much depends on the type of car you are driving, its braking efficiency, the track surface conditions and so forth, which, in effect, places the responsibility squarely with the driver. What needs to be understood is that your actions will be under close scrutiny and could be challenged by race observers. In cases of doubt, Clerks of the Course are advised by the RACMSA to consult the timekeeper to ascertain if the lap times reflected a reduction in speed following the display of a yellow flag.

A recent addition to the regulations in 1993 was the provision of a hazard sign to indicate the continuance of a static danger on the circuit, indicated on preceding laps by a yellow flag having been shown. This sign therefore frees the yellow flag, which can then be used to bring any new dangers to the attention of drivers.

Yellow flag with red stripes
If held stationary this flag warns of a slippery surface ahead,

usually because of a competitor leaking oil or petrol onto the circuit. Inevitably, any spillage is likely to be on the racing line, so you should be prepared to take avoiding action if possible. On a dry track it may be possible to see the oil, depending on how the incident occurred. It will usually appear as a shiny line if the oil is gradually being lost from an engine or a gearbox, or as a distinct patch if the oil has been 'dumped' through mechanical failure. If the area affected is extensive, be prepared to correct your steering as the car loses traction and slides, or so as to avoid other competitors, who may also be in difficulties. When the flag is waved, you are being warned that the dangerous part of the track is imminent. On following laps, even if the flag is not held out, you should still be cautious at the particular point of the circuit where the incident occurred.

Green flag

Following a danger area controlled by yellow flags, a green flag will indicate that the relevant hazard no longer applies and that racing can recommence. You will also see a green flag being shown at each marshal's post on the first lap of the practice session and on the formation lap. It is in your interest to note where they are.

Red flag

The red flag signals that the race has had to be stopped – usually because of an accident – and you should immediately slow down from racing speed, keep station with other cars and, looking out for any incident ahead, be ready to stop.

Black flag, orange disc and white number

All black flags are usually shown at the start/finish line and their colour is indicatively ominous for the recipient. If your number is shown on this particular flag you are being warned of a mechanical failure or fire, of which you may be unaware. This may be relatively minor – such as a loose rear bumper – or more serious, such as a fire in the engine bay unapparent to the driver if the flames are streaking underneath the car. Whatever the problem, once the flag is shown you are obliged to enter the pits on the next lap for necessary remedial action.

Black-and-white rectangular flag with white number

If your number is displayed on this flag it is a warning that your driving behaviour has been reported by observers as suspect and that any further instances will lead to your exclusion from the race. Only you are in a position to know the particular incident, but common indiscretions – although not considered as such by many drivers – are those of cutting corners and the cardinal but oft-quoted sin of 'overtaking under a yellow'. Whatever you have done, you have been clearly warned and continuation will invoke the next flag to be shown.

Black flag with white number

If your number is shown on this flag you are obliged to pull into the pits within one lap and report to the Clerk of the Course. If you have received no previous warning that your driving was being observed, it is probable that you have been black-flagged for a single, but serious action, which is likely to be driving considered to be dangerous, or failing to observe flags and acting accordingly.

Black-and-white chequered flag

The end of the race!

Pit etiquette

Perhaps because they are neither track nor paddock, the pit areas of most circuits are abused equally by driver and spectator alike, despite the good intentions of officials. Spectators tend to forget they are in an area where machinery can be moving at an extremely rapid speed and often cannot be seen or heard until too late, where oil and water form a slippery surface underfoot and petrol and other highly inflammable substances abound. If you consider that such areas would constitute serious breaches of Health and Safety regulations if they existed in a workplace, it is surprising sometimes that more accidents do not happen in the pit area.

Similarly, drivers conveniently tend to forget that the pit area is not part of the track and often speed down the pit lane with no chance of stopping should another car pull out or someone step across.

The general rules regarding the pit areas are contained in the Final Instructions, but will include:

• Generally only two people being allowed in the pit area to assist the driver. No children are permitted below 16 years of age, even if they do look older, so this should also be borne in mind as motor racing does tend to be a family affair. The number of passes for the pit crew will probably be restricted, especially at larger meetings.

• All petrol being stored in clearly marked containers and limited to a maximum of 5 gallons. (Note: unless specifically allowed, no refuelling shall be allowed during the race.)

• All drivers making themselves familiar with the entry and exit arrangements in the pits and keeping to a reasonable speed through the pit lane. When inbound, make sure that you signal your intentions by remaining on the appropriate side of the circuit and raising your right hand aloft. When exiting it is likely that you will be governed by lights or a flag signal. Ignore these at great personal risk and the possibility of disciplinary action by the Clerk of the Course.

Mechanical failure

When everything is running right, with the engine in full song and you cannot seem to put a tyre wrong, all of those hours of effort and the expense suddenly become worthwhile. Treasure those moments, though, because it is likely they will be matched by occasions, particularly during your formative seasons, when you will drive like a lemon and the car will seem hell-bent on not even getting off the trailer, let alone racing.

Along with your determination and willingness to succeed, you must also recognize that the ability to know when to stop is equally as valuable. This is sometimes extremely difficult when, in the heat of the moment, winning or crossing the line becomes the single most important objective in the world, but a degree of reason is needed to ensure your safety as well as preventing unnecessary expense. By all means limp home on three cylinders for the last race of the season to get enough points for a place, but there is no need to employ such heroic gestures in your first races.

The most obvious signal that you may be suffering from a mechanical failure, is a marshal holding up a black flag with an orange disc that bears your race number, as previously described. That apart, what are the warning signs you may notice in the car and what will they tell you? The following examples and diagnoses should prepare you for the worst:

Instruments

Your instrumentation, if comprehensive and accurate, is likely to provide you with the first indication that there is something awry with the engine and cooling system, which emphasizes the need for constant, albeit cursory, checks. As already detailed, orientating any analogue dial gauges so that normal readings are vertical will assist this, as will the provision of early warning lights. Generally, any slight variation in oil pressure or water temperature should be closely monitored, and obviously these are the first gauges to be checked should you suspect overheating.

Low oil pressure, depending on your particular engine, may not be terminal, but is certainly not healthy and could mean oil loss which may not be immediately obvious. But it could cause smoking or sudden main or big-end bearing failure, which may already have been hinted at through a fluctuating pressure in previous races. It will usually be self-evident anyway from the loud clattering noise coming from the engine bay and the sudden marked lack of power.

A glowing ignition warning light may not be a problem if all it indicates is that your alternator/regulator is faulty or the belt is slipping at high revs, but if the belt itself has broken or come off your race is over as this usually also drives the water pump – so a sharp rise in water temperature will be evident.

Noises and smells
It is quite difficult to hear well when wearing a balaclava and helmet, and even more so if the car is open-topped or stripped-out and therefore particularly resonant. That said, it is surprising how any sounds that are different from normal are picked up, especially if you are familiar with your car and its particular rattles and noises. When racing, the whole car is working very hard and a degree of noise is to be expected, but you should also be paying attention to unusual or unfamiliar sounds.

Unusual noises are not the only warning signs that something is wrong as some faults are silent and a strange smell in the cockpit – emanating from the car I might add! – may be all you have to alert you of an impending failure.

Perhaps the most serious of any odours is that which indicates an on-board fire, but this need not be the case in all circumstances. A small loss of oil on a hot exhaust will produce an immense amount of smoke and this is likely to find its way into the car no matter how well the bulkhead has been sealed. Similarly, what you may in fact be smelling is the problem another car is having in front of you. Therefore, although you should be prepared for swift and timely action, do not panic and set off the extinguisher because you suspect an engine bay fire – if you do have one there will be no doubt about it.

Fires that can be attributed to electrical faults and short-circuits are unfortunately a relatively common and unforgivable occurrence. In most cases they can be traced back to poor connections, wiring chafing on sharp edges or inadequate fusing, all of which should never have been allowed to happen through good preparation. They are accompanied by a very acrid smell and may cause the loss of power, instruments and lead to a more serious fire occurring.

The most pungent and readily identifiable smell is that associated with the braking system. Under severe braking the pads/shoes will become very hot, which is not a problem unless they glaze over or transfer such heat to the brake fluid which, under pressure, can boil, leading to excess pedal travel and so on. If you notice the very unique smell associated with these braking problems you should examine your braking system closely after the race and consider whether there is sufficient venting and if you need to change to a better fluid or brake material. In the race itself there is very little that you can do if you suffer total brake failure other than to retire, but if suffering from brake fade you can usually continue. Brake fade is normally apparent as excessive pedal travel if the brake fluid is getting hotter than its boiling point, although there may also be a general deterioration in braking power as stated above. A successive pumping action on the pedal will repressurize the brake lines and bring the pedal up close to its normal position temporarily, but there is little that can be done immediately to stop the pads from glazing. Post-race, the solution is to increase cooling ventilation. Generally, in such a situation all you can do is be aware of the reduction in braking power and drive accordingly, which may mean using the gears to reduce speed, leading to slower lap times and losing places – such is life.

CHAPTER 7

Race day

"It is all down to the fine tuning, the fine tuning of my car, its chassis and balance, and my body, my heart and my brain. To be at my peak I need to have them all together at their peaks at the same time. For me it is a task and a challenge every time I drive."
Ayrton Senna
Sunday Times, October 22, 1989

To many, motor racing evokes memories of far-off carefree days when dashing young men sporting soft caps and goggles would roar down the pit lane in open-top cars to the cheers of the crowd.

That such nostalgic images still linger in the hearts of many drivers and spectators is one of the numerous features that makes the sport so attractive. Who, for instance, cannot fail to be affected by visiting, or better still, even having the privilege of driving at motor racing circuits whose names conjure up childhood images of famous drivers and their headline-making exploits?

Over the years, however, the excitement and enthusiasm of the sport has had to be tempered by increasingly stringent safety measures, introduced to protect both the watching public and the participants. Further, with spectators used to the immediacy of television and with the increasing trend to expect instant action, organizers of race events have to ensure that the busy race schedule runs on time to prevent boredom creeping in. The recent allowance by the RACMSA for a trial 'streamlining' of race procedures with shortened practice times is therefore welcome. If successful, the trial will hopefully be developed to ensure that motor racing becomes a less bureaucratic activity.

In combination, these two criteria have resulted in rules, regulations and a procedural regime – a possibly daunting prospect for the novice who can find it difficult to grasp that such a systematic approach is necessary to get through what, after all, is supposed to be an enjoyable leisure activity. It sometimes appears that training for a Private Pilot's Licence may be a cheaper and less bureaucratic alternative.

As stated previously, the definitive guide to the safety and procedural aspects to be followed is the *RAC British Motor Sports Yearbook*, otherwise known as the *Blue Book*. This is lengthy, meticulous and – because it is essentially a rulebook – has been written in a semi-legal manner, which probably explains why it is not read as often as it should be (especially by those who would benefit most from so doing!). Despite occasional criticism that the book is not user-friendly, it is certainly comprehensive and deserves to be read in parts by all drivers, with the sections on circuit safety being absolutely essential.

So, in order to guide you smoothly through your first race day, this chapter begins by setting out some of the main formal procedures you will need to follow; it would be a shame, for instance, if you were excluded for not having a current club card, or because you were not aware when you must report to the Clerk of the Course. Undoubtedly, from time to time some newcomers will view the officialdom that accompanies motor racing as being petty or even obstructive, but they should remember that an unregulated sport is a disorganized and dangerous one.

There may be occasions when you will feel frustrated because the views or versions of events expressed by race officials do not accord with your own, but my advice in these circumstances is that you should try to keep calm and if necessary use the appeal mechanisms that exist for your benefit: shouting or resorting to intimidation will not work, and is likely to lead you into even more trouble.

Remember, too, that the majority of officials are unpaid, and participate merely to be close to the sport, and that without all these volunteers being prepared to give up their time each weekend, motorsport at grass-roots level would either be considerably more expensive or would not exist at all. I urge you, therefore, at least to respect their contribution and have a little more understanding of their point of view in moments of disagreement.

Signing on

Your first obligation when arriving at the circuit is to 'sign on', which is nothing more complicated than it suggests, unless you have mistakenly brought last year's licence or have forgotten it entirely. Sometimes it makes me wonder why the licences are not colour-coded each year.

At the signing-on desk you will be expected to show an up-to-date licence, valid for your class of race, and to sign your name on the relevant race sheet signifying that you intend to compete. You will also be asked if you wish to hand in your licence for signature by Race Control (you can obtain a maximum of two signatures per meeting). This is a method of recording your final race position and, assuming you finish, is proof that you did not contravene any safety requirements during the day.

These endorsing signatures are used as a simple qualification device by the RACMSA to determine whether or when you should be allowed to remove the novice's cross from your car (you require eight signatures for this), and later, for qualification for a higher class of licence to enable you to compete in major National or International events.

Remember to pick up your licence at the end of the meeting, not only out of courtesy to the organizing club, but also to remove the danger of it becoming lost; if you leave it behind and your next outing is quite soon, you have an additional unnecessary worry in that you will be without your licence until it arrives back by post.

It is usual practice at signing-on to be asked to produce an appropriate motor club membership card if the race meeting is of 'closed' status, meaning that only members of the organizing or specifically invited clubs are allowed to participate. As regards documentation at race meetings, it is sensible to keep all the paperwork together and with your kitbag. Some people use an old envelope, others their back pocket, but a clipboard is probably the best idea as it performs the dual role of keeping everything together tidily whilst 'looking the part', complete with stopwatch and sunglasses attached.

Once you have signed on you will receive a complimentary raceday programme, a scrutineering ticket and, if applicable, pit passes and last-minute information about driver meetings, alterations to the schedule and the like. At most of the larger events you will also be asked to complete a competitor's sheet, which is a standard proforma asking for any relevant details of you and your car that can be used later to good effect by the race commentator. This is the ideal opportunity to thank your sponsors, unpaid helpers and anyone else who knows you, so please take the time and trouble to complete the form with interesting and truthful information and then return it promptly to Race Control. Writing "Nude hang-gliding" in the 'Other Hobbies' section is now rather old hat, by the way.

Scrutineering

Scrutineering is a trying, but necessary task that can perhaps best be compared with the feelings you experience when visiting the dentist or the MoT station. Perhaps it is the air of expectation, or the sight of learned experts peering at your handiwork, but scrutineering always makes me nervous. This could stem from the uncertainty of not knowing whether the car will pass or fail, but it could also be associated with the loss of control as the car is being examined by someone else.

On a practical level, it does not matter that the car has been checked many times before at other circuits and passed: it is still one of those quirks of life that different scrutineers will have different interpretations of safety requirements. Some may have a bee in their (and under your) bonnet about all sorts of details that can catch you unawares and you are unlikely to be able to contest their views. Generally speaking, though, as they tend to err on the side of perfection rather than allow poorer standards, scrutineers can perhaps be forgiven for their inconsistency. For example, their close examination of your battery connections is not meant to be critical for the sake of it, but is probably derived from their experience of seeing so many cars reduced to a burnt-out shell by fires that could have been avoided.

From a more positive viewpoint, you may have checked and then double-checked the car, but an independent examination can only help to increase your confidence; besides, it is also comforting to know that all of the cars with which you will be sharing a track have been through the same rigorous procedure.

In your Final Instructions, which are usually posted to you during the previous week, you will have been given a time band during which you are expected to have the car scrutineered. Although the norm these days seems to be not to get there until the queue starts, this is not to be recommended if you are down for the first race, which usually means the first practice session, when panic can easily set in at the sight of a seemingly never-ending line of cars. It therefore pays to be early and at the head of the queue.

As emphasized in other chapters, attention to detail is vitally important and perhaps even more so in the scrutineering bay, where safety is paramount. The advice of someone who prepares or races the same car as you is also invaluable in this regard, as is methodically reading through the technical regulations that apply to your race series. I am particularly indebted to Mike Garton, one of the country's leading sports and industry consultants and a chief scrutineer himself, for providing me with a list of common problems encountered by scrutineers, and this is set out below.

Although there will probably be additional areas to which you should devote your attention, if you take heed of the points raised you are less likely to cause delay at the head of the queue and to be able to enjoy your motorsport safely and with confidence.

Scrutineering – a checklist
Presentation Always present the car in a clean and tidy state, which means no old rust or loose bits of trim. It is also common to find nuts, bolts and tools lying under the bonnet and in the footwell, so take care to check these areas.

Controls The steering wheel, column and track rod ends

should have no play and the pedals and cables should be secure.

Brackets All additional metalwork such as brackets for instruments, switches and so on, should have a rolled finish (no sharp or jagged edges) and be fixed securely, not just taped up.

Isolator switches These should be regularly maintained and lubricated as a dry joint will be ineffective. All cable pulls to isolators and extinguishers should be checked similarly and any kinks or tight bends avoided.

Wiring All wiring should be neatly loomed and any bare wires insulated. It only takes a few minutes with a roll of insulating tape to transform some engine bays.

Windows Clean all of the windows and ensure that there are no old stickers and labels. Also remember that the only scrutineering ticket that should be shown is the one valid for that race meeting.

Battery This should be securely fastened, with the earth lead taped or bound in yellow for identification purposes. If the battery is situated in the cockpit it must be contained in a non-conductive sealed box.

Fire extinguisher You can use the absolute minimum permitted – it's your life – but a better alternative is to fit a plumbed-in system discharging into both the engine bay and the cockpit footwell. Whatever extinguisher is fitted must be secure and you should not just rely on the clips provided – in an impact a loose extinguisher is a lethal weapon.

Fuel tank/pump/lines If the tank is non-standard it should be secure and not simply supported by a slotted angle and a few rubber grommets. The end of the breather pipe should be terminated below the bottom of the tank so that whatever way the car ends up, the fuel will not be lost.

The fuel pump should also be secure and any electrical connections be of the screw-type to prevent them pulling out and causing a short-circuit. If the pump is fitted in the boot, make sure that there is adequate drainage in case of spillage.

Any replacement fuel lines should be of the Aeroquip type and fitted with screw connections – and *only* of this type and of one length if in the cockpit.

Brakes These should generally be clean with sound hoses, no leaks evident and with the correct brake fluid levels. Pads should have an adequate level of wear remaining.

Wheels These should be of the correct, preferably open, type to allow the extent of stud penetration to be seen. As steel wheels become older, and having been removed and refitted many times, the areas beneath the wheelnuts tend to crush. This can result in a wheel flying off even though the wheelnuts are tight – in fact probably too tight – so use a torque wrench. If you have alloy wheels these should be checked closely at regular intervals for any hairline cracks.

Clothing All items of clothing must comply to the latest standards and you should look after them. Helmets especially should be protected well when not being used and should not be presented tatty and scratched. They should always have the RACMSA sticker in place. Wear Nomex or soft leather boots, not plastic trainers.

A simple, but effective method of showing the scrutineer that you are organized is to set out your race clothing for easy inspection on your passenger seat or on the boot floor rather than watch him half-heartedly remove them from your sports bag. Such discipline will also ensure that you actually remember to take all of your kit.

If your car is approved, the scrutineer will sign the ticket handed to you earlier. You should then affix this in the window behind the driver's seat where it can be seen clearly – most drivers then use this as a pocket arrangement for future tickets, which is fine as long as only the valid ticket is visible. This ticket will be checked later by another marshal when you are in the collection area ready to go out onto the circuit, hence the need for it to be on the car and not buried in your kitbag back in the paddock.

If there are any problems with your car, the scrutineer will note down and advise you of the relevant defects and the car will have to be presented again. This is another good reason for getting there early to allow for such remedial work to be carried out in good time, particularly in your first season when your handiwork may not be to the collective standards required at various circuits. From experience it generally seems to take at least a complete season to 'shake down' the car and make all the modifications needed to satisfy all of the scrutineers all of the time.

Occasionally, the scrutineer will make observations that are not serious, but may be for your long-term benefit, such as drawing your attention to a pipe or wire that may be chafing in the engine bay. In this instance it is worth noting down these points and taking prompt action because you are likely to forget them as soon as you leave the bay and realize the ordeal is over. Failure to do so usually means the potential defect coming back to haunt you later, so it is a good idea to have your trusty clipboard or notebook handy. Similarly, if there is anything that you promise faithfully to undertake before you go out to practice, such as retaping the lights, note them down and attend to them straightaway – it is surprising how many scrutineers are seen later walking up and down the grid making final checks. If they recognize your car and decide to check whether you fulfilled your earlier promises you had better be sure that you did.

Clerk of the Course

If this is your first time racing at the circuit you are obliged to report to the Clerk of the Course, usually at a pre-determined time set out in your Final Instructions, which is generally after scrutineering, but always before your practice session. There you will be briefed, not necessarily by the Clerk of the Course, but perhaps by one of his deputies, on some of the circuits aspects that may catch you unawares, so it is in your best interests to listen. Following this, you will usually be subjected to an impromptu test on safety, which involves identifying some of the various warning flags you will encounter later in the day, explaining what they mean and what you must do. This should pose no trouble at all to anyone who has had the sense to memorize them from the *RAC Blue Book*; the incentive to do so should be the likelihood of not racing if you fail to give the correct answers, in addition to the public humiliation you would face.

Aside from these formal aspects, this is the ideal time to ask questions of someone who will be ably qualified to answer them and pleased to do so. For example, if you are unsure of the signalling procedure for exiting the pits, then ask – it will be toc late when you are faced with the problem in a race situation.

Finally, remember that Clerks of the Course are very busy people and almost obliged to view you as an idiot and a potential liability until you prove otherwise, so try not to view their occasionally brusque manner as insulting. If you are unwise and ignore their advice, or transgress any of the safety requirements, do not be surprised if your name is read out over the public address system with instructions to report to their office. Even a mild rebuke is an event to be dreaded, especially as most Clerks of the Course have this habit of performing their function at other meetings, and you will not be forgotten: you can run, but you cannot hide. Serious contraventions may result in disciplinary action that could mean a fine or the suspension of your racing licence.

Drivers' briefings

One final procedure of which you need to be aware is the drivers' briefing. These are not necessarily held at every meeting, but when they are it is important that you attend. Failure to do so means that you will not be racing and occasionally it has been known for competitors to be asked to sign as they leave as proof of attendance. So, you have been warned.

Briefings are normally held at the completion of the practice sessions, before or during lunch, and usually in the scrutineering bay. Their main thrust is to emphasize the need for safety and clarify any special requirements for races involving split-grids, driver changes, or the like, but frequently they are also used by the organizing club as another opportunity to raise the subject of safety and to stress its importance. This also neatly allows the matter of sportsmanship to be addressed, which is no bad thing. Unfortunately, for some reason this always seems to result in sheepish grins and the odd comment amongst groups of drivers, conjuring up memories of schoolboys in morning assembly.

It is a sad fact that in recent years the standard of sportsmanship has been seen to have declined, no more evidently than in the regular 'demolition derby' witnessed on television during so many rounds of the British Touring Car Championship. The worry is that such a decline in standards at a professional level can have a detrimental influence on the behaviour of drivers competing in amateur events, or even distort their understanding of what constitutes acceptable behaviour and what does not.

I remember in particular a round of the BTCC at Pembrey in 1993, when Andy Rouse, one of the foremost and respected drivers in the series, was forced to retire his Ford Mondeo which was making its debut in the championship. Before covering the race, the TV programme had concentrated on the preparation work that had gone into the car and the viewer saw the completed vehicle in its attractive livery next to a sponsor's lorry. Then, almost from the green light, the car was bumped and barged repeatedly until finally, whilst lying third, the bodywork was damaged so much as to foul the tyres. After the race Rouse was heard to say that he had "...come here for the motor racing, not stock car racing." As I write he has recently announced his retirement from being a competitor.

Unfortunately, although such carnage may make 'good television', it does nothing for the image of the sport or for the perceived skill or behaviour of its participants, and to anyone setting out in motor racing I would earnest recommend that they put to the back of their mind the sort of driving tactics they may have witnessed on 'the box', and pay due regard to the warnings of Clerks of the Course and other race officials as to the penalities, let alone the dangers, they will risk through overly aggressive driving. A phrase often heard in the paddock, which perhaps best sums up the need to keep competition and rivalry within reasonable bounds, is: "We've all got to go to work on Monday." It's something worth remembering.

Practice

First race practice for the complete novice can quite easily involve just 10 or 15 minutes of track time, all of it spent trying to become familiar with the circuit layout and even getting acquainted with the basic handling characteristics of the car itself. It is therefore not surprising when such a brief session ends with a frustratingly poor lap time and a position towards the back of the grid.

With an inevitably tight budget, previous testing on the circuit is unlikely to have been possible, and if time has been a similarly precious commodity the car will probably only have been ready to race just a few days before the meeting.

The better prepared driver, however, will already have had an advantage on arrival at the circuit, even if this is his first visit, as he will have examined the layout, albeit on paper, become familiar with the names of each corner and read the Final Instructions thoroughly. Apart from important information on the timetable for the day and safety procedures to be followed, these often contain particular quirks relevant to the circuit, which can easily be overlooked and consequently transgressed.

A typical example which springs to mind is the probability of being black-flagged at Brands Hatch for going wide on more than one occasion at the bottom of Paddock Hill Bend onto what is known as the 'Old Circuit'. This, to the uninformed, looks simply like a different shade of Tarmacadam, but if you are summoned by the Clerk of the Course your ignorance of its true origin may well be construed as arrogance as it is clearly mentioned in the Final Instructions and is particularly emphasized at the initial meeting with the Clerk of the Course. If you find this hard to believe, the next time you visit the circuit, watch the marshal, at the bottom of the hill, note and telephone through the competition numbers of each culprit.

Of course, you may be one of those rare animals sometimes known as 'natural drivers', who are so self-assured and talented that such minutiae seem unimportant. However, for the rest of us, paying attention to such details will hopefully provide an advantage over other drivers at no cost and contribute to a professional approach that is more often seen in the winning team.

Practice preparation

Wherever possible, try to take advantage of the opportunity to walk the circuit earlier in the day: it is surprising how much you will discover, even if you have raced there before, as the track layout may have been changed slightly during the winter months. Also, any interim track maintenance or, more frequently, the lack of it, may have a marked effect on surface adhesion and consequently the handling of your car.

Early mornings may not be your forte, but hopefully a clear track and mind will help to focus your attention on the day ahead. Race day is so busy that this will be one of the few times you will be able to collect your thoughts. If you leave it too late, do not be surprised if much of the track is filled with your peers or has been closed by the course officials in readiness for the first practice session.

Walking from the start line, assess the possibilities of overtaking whilst taking into account the all-important first corner. Here is where you, and therefore your fellow competitors, will probably be at their most nervous and liable to make a mistake, so think about the options that may be open to you. Look up at the gantry holding the start lights and try to imagine the race for that first corner. It will be hot and noisy, as it always is, and there will be cars on all sides weaving and jostling for position. Everyone will be braking as late as possible and trying for the inside line. This should provide additional motivation for the practice session as, of course, your performance will determine your grid position. Where do you hope to be?

When walking round, remember that unless you are unusually short in stature you will be looking at the track from far higher a position than when actually sitting in your car, so take time to stop occasionally and crouch down, particularly at approaches to corner sections. This will give you a true impression of how they will look when you practice and race.

Criss-crossing most of the circuit will be numerous tyre marks, which will each have stories to tell – some of bravery and some of stupidity. When they appear on corners these marks may give a good indication of how difficult each one is and provide graphic evidence of previous mistakes that you will not wish to repeat. With experience you will be able to differentiate between the marks left by motorcycles, sidecar combinations and, of more interest to you, cars.

One of the most surprising aspects of which you will be aware is the amount of debris lying about despite the best intentions of marshals. You will also see that dust, mixed with the residue of rubber scrubbed off tyres, will accumulate, particularly on parts of the track that are off the usual racing line. Due to the lack of adhesion offered, these parts of the track are aptly called 'the marbles,' and should it rain will become very slippery indeed.

Although you should try to keep on the racing line, which is swept clean by traffic, you may need to drive onto this surface if the track suddenly becomes congested, avoiding action is necessary, or you want to overtake.

'Reading' a track is not a secret, but simply a matter of observation and common sense, which you will gradually acquire as you become more experienced. It is relatively easy to identify changes in camber, undulations and where the surface is rippling or breaking up because of frequent braking. These areas, as they become more distressed, are often broken out and replaced with a material with different grip from the main track.

Less obvious, sometimes, are the hidden dangers that will only become apparent when you are driving on the limit, such as the area of track under the trees on the farmhouse part of the circuit at Cadwell Park. This always seems to remain damp and can cause an imbalance as one side of the car loses traction as you accelerate downhill from the slow bend. Similarly, look closely at the high and often jagged edges of 'rumble strips' at countless circuits. These are intended to dissuade you from encroaching too far on the inside of the corner and they fulfil their function well, but at a cost. If your car is low, and most race cars are, it is fairly easy to damage the suspension or even catch the engine sump, not to mention the effect on your tyres. At Snetterton, I once witnessed a car losing a wheel at Russell's as the driver locked up, went over the gravel and clipped the back of the rumble strip.

As you become more experienced you will also be able to distinguish between the safe run-off areas and those that are deeply rutted or marshy due to poor drainage – put a tyre wrong there and you could easily flip the car onto its roof. In the interests of safety many tracks are making gravel-type traps literally that, by increasing their depth and breadth. Now, if you fall off into the gravel you are safe, but probably stuck unless you are fortunate enough to keep your momentum. For this reason, do not ever try to drive over a gravel trap if, for instance, you spin and end up facing the wrong way – it will not work, believe me.

Whilst walking around the circuit, try to note the position of the marshals' posts as it will be too late should you have the misfortune to suffer an engine fire and need their help. If you are unfortunate enough to have a fire on board it is better that you save time by driving up to them rather than waiting for them to get to you. During the race these posts will also be staffed by observers and flag marshals. The former will be there, as the name suggests, to watch for any driver misdemeanours which, if serious, can be reported immediately back to Race Control over two-way radio or telephone. This category would include the reporting of any dangerous driving or a car so damaged that it could endanger the driver or others. In both instances the relevant car would be flagged-in, although the driver concerned would receive quite different receptions. Less serious offences are noted, reported to the Clerk of the Course after the race, and could involve disciplinary action being taken.

Last, but not least, familiarize yourself with the pit area and in particular the entry and exit positions, not only in case you have to use them, but also so that you know precisely where other cars may be leaving or rejoining the circuit. At the same time you should also note whether exit control lights are to be used, or whether a flag marshal will wave you out instead. Whilst in the pits, try to visualize exactly where you would need to pull up – a flat tyre is not uncommon and an engine fire may be rare, but it could happen – and yes, it will probably happen to you.

The exact spot will be determined by where your pit crew is situated and this is a matter to be discussed with your timekeeper/signaller. Ideally, the best place for them to be on the pit wall is next to some natural landmark such as a prominent stanchion or advertising hoarding as this will be easier to locate from the track when you are travelling at speed.

A final tip is to make time to chat to some of the stewards of the meeting. As enthusiasts, and probably officiating at their home circuit, they will generally be only too pleased to pass on some of the knowledge they have gained over the years, and their advice could well mean that all-important tenths of a second can be clipped from your lap times.

So, having completed a lap and returned to the start line you should, by now, have a fairly good impression of the circuit and at least be forewarned of some of its more difficult parts. If you are still unsure about certain aspects, why not walk the circuit again? Race cars are weighed without the driver, so the exercise may do you good in more ways than one.

Assuming that you have meticulously examined the car since its last outing – yes, failure to do this most obvious of tasks is still common – you will probably only need to make sure the car is clean and polished. It is surprising how common it is for cars that have had small fortunes lavished on their engine, suspension and bodywork to be seen on the grid covered in oil and grime from the journey to the meeting, if not the previous event some two weeks ago.

There is no excuse for having a dirty car, even if it is race-damaged, and I will go as far as to state that a car's poor condition will have an adverse effect on the driver. A clean and polished car shows care and this will ease the driver's mind, who will be reassured that such attention to detail has similarly been spent on the mechanical parts of it. An unquestioning faith in the car's reliability and safety will be a positive asset during the race, enabling the driver to think of more pressing issues like driving to win.

When seated in the car it is easy to make the mistake of simply adjusting the shoulder straps as these are readily at hand, but this tends to pull the lap belt too high so that it rests over your stomach. In practice this belt should be lower, passing over the waist and holding the hips firmly at the side and down into the seat. Always adjust the lap belt tension via the buckles on either side of the base of the seat, then the shoulder straps, before finally adjusting the rear straps. Do not over-tighten the shoulder straps as they will pull down unnecessarily on your shoulders, press down on your chest and generally become uncomfortable. The harness is there to secure you, not strangle you, so make sure you can breathe deeply without trouble and have a reasonable degree of movement, and check that you can turn the wheel easily and reach all the switches you will need. If you are struggling to do any of these it is likely that your seat is also incorrectly adjusted. Naturally, all of this should have been sorted out well before the day of the race, and is one of many items that will be picked up in any testing you carry out.

Last-minute checks should really be for your own peace of mind, but one that is often forgotten is to assume your normal driving position and with the help of an assistant, adjust the wing mirrors. They will probably have been knocked and moved out of position since your last outing and once you are strapped in you will be unable to alter them.

Setting a time

Approximately half-an-hour before your practice session, you will be called up over the public address system to the assembly area to await the completion of the preceding session. Positioning at this stage is considered vitally important by some, who will try to set out alongside their closest rival, presumably to observe weaknesses, psyche them out and compare performance in close proximity. Do not be drawn into such situations as they usually conceal thinly-disguised attempts by some competitors to hold the race early and show off.

It really does not matter whether you are at the front, middle or back as you go out to start the session because everyone will eventually settle down to a different speed and within a few laps the initial order will have changed. It is very tempting to floor the throttle immediately, especially if you get caught up in a pack of cars, but it is best to curb your enthusiasm and settle down to a steady but sure pace. This will ensure that you gradually build up your tyres and engine to the operating temperatures at which they will work with maximum efficiency. During this initial period you can also get to know the circuit using your knowledge from walking around it earlier, taking the opportunity to experiment with a slightly different line into each corner;

the slower speed will allow this to be done with relative safety. In summary, use this warm-up period wisely and check your instruments, keep an eye on your mirrors and remember to take it easy.

A useful tip if it is your first time at the circuit is to try to follow one of the more experienced competitors for the first few laps. This will give you the benefit of seeing a more informed, although not necessarily the best, approach. Too often drivers believe it better to have a clear track ahead, but this is only generally true once you are more familiar with the circuit. Until that time it is more advantageous to have a car slightly ahead of you to act as a marker, allowing you a reference point for your speed and approach to corners.

Under the current *Blue Book* regulations you are obliged to complete at least three laps during the practice session to qualify for the race. This qualifying requirement is a safety precaution to ensure that each competitor has a basic knowledge of the track prior to being subjected to the altogether more hostile race environment.

Whilst practice may seem to be fairly processional, the novice could be left way behind in the actual race with literally no idea as to which way and at what speed to go. Admittedly this may be hard to imagine, but on a strange track, perhaps in the wet, it can often take the whole practice session just to get the line right into most of the corners, and there may well be some parts of the track that will catch out competitors for many seasons.

If you fail to complete three laps due to a mechanical failure or miss the practice session entirely, most Clerks of the Course will treat your plight sympathetically and, subject to time constraints, arrange for you to take three laps out of session, perhaps in the lunch hour. Try to give the officials as much notice as possible, however, as you may not be the only driver in this predicament and the necessary arrangements will have to be made with Race Control and the marshals around the circuit.

The penalty for practising out of session is that in the actual race you have to start at the back of the grid and be held back for 10 seconds from the green light. This will be the longest 10 seconds you have ever encountered as you sit and wait while the other cars disappear into the distance.

If you are faced with this situation, try to keep your temper and, above all, concentration. You will have the advantage of a clear line to the first and subsequent corners and you should use this wisely. Do not go too fast in your haste to catch up with the other cars as it will take at least two, or maybe three laps to do so and you will run the risk of losing control.

Back to your practice session, having steadily built up your speed and, hopefully, settled the car in with all of the instruments reading correctly, it is time to set an initial flying lap time. Leaving the preceding corner to the start/finish line at a greater speed than previously, you will be timed from the moment you cross the line. You should still be cautious at this stage, though, and not take any unnecessary risks as generally these early laps can still catch you out. It is more important for you to concentrate on what you are doing at each part of the circuit, repeating your line if it seems to be right, but taking corrective action if you are getting it all wrong.

Consistency in approaching each bend correctly at the right speed and on the right line, knowing and correcting where you are losing time, will all result in your lap times falling steadily. You should be aware of this, naturally, but a more accurate measurement will be provided by your pit crew, who will be signalling your previous lap time to you as you pass.

Whereas your position relative to other cars was unimportant at the beginning, as the session draws on, slower cars may get in your way and disrupt your rhythm and approach to bends. This is particularly noticeable in a combined allcomers/handicap race where the relative speeds of competitors may be considerably different. Therefore it becomes fairly important towards the end that you know where those slower cars are and whether they are going to disrupt you. If you become delayed, perhaps at a chicane or a bottleneck of slower cars, it is better to conserve your tyres and temper, edge off the power for the remainder of the lap and prepare for the next one. Do try to use every opportunity, however, to practice overtaking slower cars and experimenting with subtly different approaches to each corner until you get them right.

If you are in one of those slower cars, don't despair: there are too many reasons why you may be slower and you cannot be expected to evaluate them on the track. If yours is proving to be just a marginally slower car, try to use the faster cars to your advantage and slipstream one, if possible, on exiting a corner at the beginning of a long straight. This tactic is quite useful towards the end of the session as relative speeds increase, and is described more fully later.

Throughout the session, with the aid of a pit board, your timekeeper should give you your lap time as you pass the pits. Remember that this relates to the previous lap and not the one that you are completing. Other useful information that can be relayed to you is the number of minutes left in the session, the relative difference between your lap time and a close rival or a previous personal best time – all of these will need to be agreed in advance, however.

On completion of the session the chequered flag will be waved at the start/finish line, after crossing which you are expected to slow down and drive steadily for a further lap as far as the entry to the pit lane. Here you will probably be ushered in for good measure by a flag marshal. At this point, if you have a speedometer fitted use it, as leaving a featureless circuit is rather like leaving a motorway exit and your sense of speed will be distorted. For this reason keep especially alert in the paddock area, as there may well be children and slower moving cars.

Elated still by adrenalin, it is very tempting at this stage to join family and friends to bask in the warm glow of your unofficial lap times, but a more practical move is to take readings of the tyre temperatures and pressures whilst they are still hot and check the engine bay for any immediate attention.

A commonly expressed view in the paddock is that you should not change anything between practice and the race, but if there are obvious small corrections that can be made to make the car handle better or be quicker, these should be carried out. Do not make dramatic changes such as realigning your wheel tracking or camber angles, though; if you feel you have major handling problems, it is best to resolve these at a later testing session when incremental changes can be made and their effects measured.

Examples of obvious work that needs to be done immediately after practice – so that you do not forget – include checking fluid levels, tappet clearances and, of course, refuelling. When calculating the amount of fuel you will need it is best to err on the side of caution by taking into account the possibility of the race being stopped and restarted, but remember that a full tank may cause spillage during hard cornering. Anyway, it is all added weight, and that will only make the car slower.

Ideally, the time after practice should also be used to reflect on the parts of the track where you were confident, then concentrate your mind on those sections where you need to go more quickly. Whilst such thoughts are most productively made in isolation, it is more likely that you will soon be found with your fellow competitors near the signing-on area, waiting for the release of the official lap times and confirmation of your place on the grid. This is the moment of truth, when you will see all of your hard work converted into time, and mere fractions of a second will separate a handful of cars.

Concentration

Driving "at 10/10ths" or "on the limit" are phrases commonly overheard in racing circles, but are usually describing no more than someone making a little more effort than normal or driving unsafely, and probably beyond their ability. To drive truly at the limit, though, you have to know just what that limit is, which is not only what the car can achieve, but also the extent of your own driving capabilities. To compete and win requires total concentration on the part of the driver, even in short sprint events, let alone for the length of time of a typical 10-lap circuit race.

It is difficult to explain how to improve something as cerebral as concentration, but the main aim is to increase and maintain self-confidence, which is a very personal trait, and in all cases will be assisted by meticulous preparation in its various forms, as discussed previously.

In the hustle and bustle of raceday it is quite easy to 'forget to think' and spend so much time talking, watching and doing that you are distracted from applying any concentration to your imminent race. If possible, try to set aside some time during the day, preferably after practice, to be on your own and consider your lap times in comparison with those of your fellow competitors, where you are on the grid, your possible race tactics and so forth. You cannot switch on concentration like a tap, so you owe it to yourself to create time and use it wisely, because it is another element of your preparation.

Surprisingly, concentration on the track is an area that is either overlooked or given insufficient thought by some competitors. If you suddenly find yourself remote from others on the circuit it is so easy to relax and start to drive more conservatively – after all, what is the point in racing if there is no-one to race with? However, if during your race you find yourself in this position it is essential that you continue to compete. This will be best achieved by setting yourself targets to replace the temporarily absent fellow competitors, the most obvious of which being to reduce your lap times. On a more tangible level, though, be prepared to sustain your concentration by attacking each bend to the very best of your ability and gradually 'reeling in' the car in front, however far ahead it may be.

Above all, do not give up. It would be easy at this point to become despondent, particularly if you are a novice, but try to keep matters in perspective and remember that this is supposed to be enjoyable. Also, from experience, your fastest lap during the race will be at least two or three seconds quicker than you managed in practice because you are more psyched up and will be in direct competition with the rest of the cars around you. It is also worth remembering that your final placing in the race will have as much to do with judgment, reliability and luck as speed. One missed gear or a mysterious misfire will have more of a bearing than the difference of a tenth of a second between you and your nearest rival. Think positively.

In the short time between the end of your practice session and the race you may be able to observe other sessions in progress. By situating yourself at one of the more difficult parts of the circuit you will be able to see how other drivers, albeit probably in different cars from your own, enter and exit the corner. This may help, but try not to be put off if you witness someone getting it wrong and coming to grief.

If your race is later in the programme you may also be able to see some of the earlier ones in progress – which is an added bonus. A useful tip here is to watch the starts and count how long the cars are held on the line waiting for the lights to change from red to green. If a trend emerges it may help you later.

Eventually the cars in the race preceding yours will line up on the grid and following the distant screech of tyres there will be a public address announcement calling your race to the assembly area.

CHAPTER 8

The race

"When the flag drops, the bullshit stops."
Frank Gardner
Attributed

You have at last reached the point towards which all of your time, effort and money has been directed – your race! It does not matter whether you are about to compete in front of a capacity crowd at Silverstone on August Bank Holiday or at a cold and windswept Cadwell Park at the tail-end of the season: nothing can remove that wonderful atmosphere of expectation.

Assembly
The normal procedure is to be checked into the assembly area and lined up in grid order, this of course having been determined by everybody's fastest lap time during the official practice earlier in the day. Now is the time for drivers to begin the ritual of donning balaclava, helmet and

gloves and carrying out any last-minute preparations. Whilst this is largely a repeat of the procedure undertaken prior to practice, the atmosphere understandably tends to be a little more fraught now with the prospect of the race ahead and all that is at stake.

Some drivers will be seen chatting nervously about anything to anyone, whilst others will stroll around confidently trying to psyche-out the opposition. It is up to you which method you choose to calm your nerves, but try not to take it all so seriously that you forget to enjoy yourself – it is supposed to be fun, you know!

Hopefully you will have taken your time in carrying out your pre-race preparations because rushing around can so often lead to errors such as forgetting to refuel the car, checking the tyre pressures or leaving bodywork catches undone.

Once 'kitted up', settle yourself into the car in good time and, if it is wet, wipe the soles of your race boots dry (keep a rag handy in the car for this). Then, preferably with some assistance, fasten up your harness, checking each strap individually for tension and make sure that there are no flapping ends to distract you later.

Once strapped in, last-minute checks with your pit crew and final adjustments of your mirrors should be all that are needed to make you race-ready. When making these final checks take special care to arm the extinguisher by removing the lock pin and to search for any loose items such as tools, or even a race programme, lying around in the car as these can be potentially lethal if they get thrown around in the race. Even if a spanner does not end up under your brake pedal it is a distraction just knowing that it might. Psychologically, at this late stage it is reassuring to have someone fussing over these tiny details to the car as such care and attention helps to instill confidence. Finally, if it is warm weather, keep your door open until the last moment so as to keep the car as cool as possible; on very hot and sunny days shading the windows of the car in the paddock before the race can also be beneficial.

Difficult though it may be, now is the time to relax and shut yourself off from the events around you. You must try not to be overcome by the occasion as nervousness can easily lead to mistakes, but conversely you should not be cocky as this can lead to over-confidence. The phrase many sports personalities use in interviews before the big event is "quietly confident", and this perhaps best describes the mood to which you should aspire.

As touched on earlier, each driver has (his) own way of combating pre-race nerves. One of the most effective methods is to try to regulate your breathing, taking in slow, deep breaths through the nose and then steadily exhaling from the mouth. This technique, tried and tested in many sports, will really help to calm your nerves and banish any collywobbles.

At this stage, thinking about the race ahead is not difficult as it is only a matter of minutes away, but applied concentration is less easy. It may help to recall details of your walk around the circuit earlier in the day and the subsequent practice session, and to ask yourself such questions as: What line should I take on the corner that gives me most concern? What part of the circuit is best for overtaking? Which competitors are around me on the grid? Are they known for their acceleration off the line or was my last start better? How well you perform in the race will hinge on you getting your head together beforehand.

Mulling over these issues will help to focus your mind and while away the time usefully until, a few minutes before you are due to be called out as the previous race draws to a close, you can fire up the engine. Avoid the urge to keep over-revving it, but do keep the revs well above idle speed so as to prevent the plugs from fouling up and to help build the engine up to race temperature. You should see your water/oil gauges gradually move to their normal position, indicating that this has been achieved and that any cooling fan fitted will have cut in at the appropriate temperature.

Whilst the previous race winner is completing a victory lap of honour, the marshals will be clearing the track of any debris and towing away any cars that may have pulled off the circuit during the race and bringing them back to the paddock area. Then the course car will make a slow tour of the circuit for officials to check that all is well, the barrier will be lifted and the marshal will signal with a circular motion that you are to move out onto the track.

Starting procedures

There are two methods used to start a race, the rolling start and the standing start. Rolling starts are not the norm in the UK, but they do tend to be used for races involving turbo-engined cars, which are very prone to overheating if required to sit idling for any length of time, as well as for non-gearbox karts – for obvious reasons. Due to the increased coverage of IndyCar racing in recent years, you are probably aware of the procedure, which generally entails leaving the assembly area in grid order behind the course pace car, completing a formation lap – confusingly also called by some a parade, green-flag or warm-up lap – two abreast until the start/finish straight. Here the pace car will peel off into the pit lane, leaving the cars to begin racing as the green starting flag is waved from the gantry on the start/finish straight.

At this point it is perhaps worth differentiating between *parade*, *pace* and *safety* cars, as each perform separate functions and the regulations governing their use have been substantially revised in recent years. A *parade* car is one that controls the formation lap prior to a standing start; a *pace* car leads the grid on the formation lap of a rolling start; and a *safety* car is used to control or neutralize a race following the partial blockage of the track or a situation where the danger is such that the yellow flag is deemed inadequate.

Due to their differing functions, these are often separate cars, although safety and pace cars can be one and the same, depending on how they are used. You are advised to read the relevant section in the *Blue Book* and your Final Instructions to determine how each car will be used, as such familiarization is vital.

The standing start is a far more common and traditional method and so is covered in more detail. Depending on whether the assembly area is before or after the start/finish line, you may end up with a short distance (as at Pembrey) or almost a complete lap (such as at Donington Park) before you form up on the grid. Once directed by marshals to your correct slot, look to each side of the track and try to select a landmark to help you fix your position when you return to the grid for the start of the race. This could be a change in the track surface or a particular advertising hoarding, for instance; although each grid position is numbered, it is far easier to be able to refer to something more obvious alongside the track.

Then, keep the engine ticking over, continue to monitor the temperature gauge and, as before, if the weather is warm, take the opportunity to open your door to help to keep the interior cool.

During this period marshals will usually be seen walking up and down the grid of cars, making last-minute checks that you are strapped in properly, have shut your windows, removed the extinguisher disarming pin and so on. They will also be checking for any signs of cars leaking excess fluids onto the track, which would prevent those unfortunates from participating further – an experience which, once witnessed, brings home quite forcibly the need for methodical care and attention in the engine bay.

I can recall one of my first races when a marshal walking along the grid of cars suddenly stopped ahead of me, crouched down and looked at the underside pensively. Immediately, having had problems in practice with oil leaking at the junction of the engine and gearbox, I had visions of more oil spilling out onto the track and thought that my race was over before it had even begun. Then he walked over slowly, stopped, leant his head into the doorway and cheerily informed me that he had just bought his wife a car like mine and asked what size of tyres I had fitted!

Generally, unless there is a problem with one of the cars being unable to start, the course officials will be keen to get the race under way as quickly as possible, so very soon a '2 minutes' board will be held aloft at the front of the grid indicating the time remaining before the formation lap begins. Similar boards will subsequently be shown, and occasionally accompanied by a klaxon, indicating when a minute and finally 30 seconds are left, until eventually a green flag will be waved from the gantry to start you all off.

If you encounter mechanical difficulty during this time and cannot start, signal this to the marshals by raising your right arm, and they in turn will warn other competitors of your situation with the aid of a yellow flag. If you eventually get going after the other cars have moved off you are not permitted to overtake and resume your previous position, so will have to start the race from the back of the grid.

Reserves
Should a race be oversubscribed, the organizers, at their discretion, can allow reserves to be included (usually 20 per cent of the field) on the basis that amongst an entry of around 30 cars there is a reasonable chance of someone having to cancel late or being unable to compete because of

trouble during practice. Reserves, although fully aware of their situation, are still in a frustrating position as they will have practised and set a lap time that could well be faster than many other cars, but this will not guarantee them a place on the grid. Instead, they have to wait, vulture-like, for someone to suffer mechanical failure or accident damage during practice so that they can take their place. If this fails to happen, the agony is prolonged by them having to take up a position at the back of the grid on the assembly lap, again waiting for someone to drop out even at this late stage. Eventually, if the cars all arrive back safely to their grid positions the reserves are obliged to leave the circuit, return to the paddock and become mere observers.

Parade lap
Back on the track, as the green flag is waved you should move off steadily behind the parade car, keeping station with the cars around you and concentrating on each corner again as you approach it. At this point your pit crew will be moved back from the pit wall to ensure their safety during the start of the race, so do not panic if you cannot see them.

Whilst on the formation lap, as in the event of you arriving late to form up on the grid, should you fall behind due to mechanical problems you will be obliged to start the race at the back alongside those cars that have practised out of session. During this lap do not wander about haphazardly, trying to warm up your tyres, as using more than half the width of the track is classified as excessive weaving and may earn you a visit to the Clerk of the Course. Also, try to remember to keep your wits about you, even at these relatively low speeds, as shunting the car in front of you before you have even started the race would be very embarrassing indeed.

As your brakes will still be cold it is also prudent to apply them early at the approaches to corners, even if this is unwarranted by your slow speed, and perhaps even to apply gentle braking with your left foot whilst you are accelerating. This is particularly helpful if you are running hard racing compounds that need considerable friction to be applied to them before they reach working temperature.

The parade car will peel off down the pit lane as you come around the final bend before the start/finish straight, and you should move over to the appropriate side of the track and slowly roll up to your grid position. This is where the previous advice about fixing a landmark becomes useful as there will no longer be any marshals on the circuit at this point to help you.

When all of the cars are finally in position, a marshal at the rear of the grid will wave a green flag as a signal to the starter – you may glimpse this in the rear-view mirror out of the corner of your eye, but do not be distracted – and a '5 seconds' board may also be held aloft – to make it perfectly clear that the race is imminent.

At this point your attention should be completely fixed on the lighting gantry and the red lights, which will remain lit for between 4 and 10 seconds before the lights are switched to green. The exact length of time before they change is arbitrary, but remember the advice earlier about watching a few other races being started before yours in case a trend emerges.

A useful tip when arriving at the grid if you are placed towards the back, is to drive up to your position slowly and with the car already in first gear. Occasionally, if the leaders have put in a fast lap and some time has elapsed since they arrived back on the grid, the flag marshal may give the all-clear signal as you are arriving and the lights may switch from red to green in quick succession. If you are still rolling in first gear, albeit slowly, you will be able to take full advantage of this situation; if you are freewheeling in neutral, however, you will almost certainly be caught out and jumped by others around you.

The start

Once the red lights come on, build up your revs to maximum (look at the tachometer as it may be so noisy in the car as to rule out gauging engine revs by sound alone) then, as the lights change to green, let out the clutch smoothly but firmly. It is difficult to describe the extent to which you should be revving the engine at the start because much will depend on your individual circumstances. As you can imagine, the term 'maximum' depends on the safe limitations of the engine and your confidence in the car's gearbox, driveshafts and so on. Many a driver has sat forlornly on the grid due to the failure of these as the rest of the pack disappear into the distance. That said, do not be afraid to rev the engine at the start as it will be enduring much more of the same during the race and a lot of revs will be needed anyway to prevent the engine stalling as the clutch bites. This is particularly applicable if you have fitted a racing clutch-plate, diaphragm and cover, which will be much fiercer than the one on the road car you used to drive to the circuit.

Clutch control is a vital element towards ensuring that you get a good start and an advantage over your fellow competitors. If you just let out the clutch pedal gradually all you will do is cause excessive wear and an acrid burning smell as you move away too slowly. At the other extreme, if you simply drop the clutch pedal in one movement you run a very high risk of breaking something critical or incurring excessive wheelspin, which again will mean a slow start. At worst you could even stall the engine, which is sacrilege! In case further encouragement were needed, any slow start or failure to start also means that you are at risk of being hit by a fast accelerating car from behind. Being firm with the clutch would appear to be the rule.

In case you are tempted to adopt a more favourable grid position by moving over to one side, creeping forwards or even jumping the lights from the standing start – or pulling ahead before crossing the start line in the case of a rolling start – be warned! Such practices are dealt with severely and if you are judged to have gained an unfair advantage over your fellow competitors you could incur a penalty of up to 10 seconds, to be added on to your eventual elapsed race time, if the race is under 30 miles distance, or up to a full minute if it over that length. The extent of the time penalty is at the discretion of the Clerk of the Course, and it can also be applied if you are deemed to be guilty of taking other unfair advantages during the race such as cutting corners. If tempted, remember that with all the cars lined up in grid formation it is very easy for the Clerk of the Course to spot one that is out of line or moves prior to the lights changing and that your actions are under close scrutiny during the race by marshals situated all around the circuit.

In addition to making a quick start, your opening moves are also critical as everyone will be hyped up and trying to attack the positions in front, so you must be able to hold your own ground. This is easier said than done in the heat of the moment, but if it is your first race you may be better off by keeping the car straight and concentrating on defending your line into the corner ahead, braking in due time and keeping out of trouble. There will be plenty of opportunities for heroics in the future and you will want your first races to go well; simply finishing would be ideal, and in some cases is an achievement in itself if the car has not been raced before.

From the moment the green light appears you must be prepared to take swift and positive action not only to avoid cars that may spin ahead of you, but also to counter the occasional sideways nudge or push, especially at the rear of the car, which can easily put you off balance. Additionally, another fairly intimidating aspect you will encounter is the funnelling of four or five cars into the space for only three. This is a true test of your resolve and self-control: to hesitate means the loss of places whereas bravery often leads to race damage and retirement. All of this, if nothing else, emphasizes the need to achieve good practice times as the nearer you are to the front the lesser the risk, especially if you have a clear track ahead of you. Motor racing is supposed to be a non-contact sport, but inevitably, with a full grid, adrenalin and a few old scores to settle, accidental knocks can easily and sometimes 'excusably' occur at the start – later on in the race is another matter, however.

As you gain more race experience, and especially if you make a point of practising them when testing, your starts should gradually improve. Being quicker off the line than the other cars, even marginally, will pay dividends in that the speed differential will enable you to edge ahead and possibly gain places even before the first corner. The way to do this is to make for the left or right of the car ahead, depending on your grid position. If on the infield side of the grid, you should look to your left to prevent the car behind from jumping into the space you covet, whereas if you are on the outfield you may well be in that position. This is easily written, but far harder to achieve in reality, and nothing will ever beat first-hand experience.

All race tactics must be dependant on your car's performance, your position on the grid, the calibre of the opposition and your own abilities and confidence, but generally you should at least be trying to maintain your position as it will have been hard-earned from the practice session.

First corners
First corners are always interesting and full of incident, so it is here, perhaps more than at any other time in the race, that

you need to be particularly aware of everything that is happening around you and prepared to react quickly to both threat and opportunity.

In the acceleration from a standing start, surrounded by other cars, relative speeds are harder to judge as your normal reference points and even the track itself cannot be seen. It is therefore not surprising to see cars 'fall off' on the outfield of the first corner (usually they have understeered off or have been pushed) or the infield (usually as a result of oversteer or, again, because they were pushed).

If you watch a grid full of accomplished racers you will see that they are all trying hard, but in the main have sufficient common sense to keep a safe distance from each other (this may well mean being separated by only a few inches, rather than the several feet considered safe in the context of normal road driving). They are exhibiting restraint, an unusual phenomenon on a race track one might think, but wholly necessary if a driver expects to remain unscathed for any length of time. In recent years we have become conditioned to the do-or-die exploits at the highest levels of the sport, but in reality it is consistency, both in trying to make each lap your best and in managing to cross the finish line in every race, which will have more of a bearing on success.

Controlled assertiveness rather than aggression is needed when racing, yet is so often overlooked on the first and subsequent bends. If in doubt, let the lunatics own the first corner, drive hard through the pieces and start racing. You will often pick up a few places due to others' early over-exuberance.

First laps
For your first laps you need to be fairly cautious as your brakes and tyres will not yet be at their best working temperature – especially if you have slicks. This is

something about which all drivers are aware, but many tend to forget in the heat of the moment as the lights change, all too often with predictable results. Above all, keep a clear head and do not brake late just because you can edge ahead by a few feet: this could be costly. That said, there is no excuse for driving too slowly as the rest of your competitors will be thinking the same, so you should exploit this! Generally, most drivers will take the first laps slower than the remainder as they settle into a steady pace and then gradually become quicker through familiarity and the heat of battle. It therefore stands to reason that if you can apply pressure at the beginning and settle into your own pace as soon as possible you will have a considerable advantage.

The key from this point on is to be able to drive to the best of your ability for the whole race, within the limitations of the car and track conditions, of course, recognizing that these can be variable and will require you to respond accordingly. Consider, for example, the loss of performance through brake fade, an occasional misfire or the effects of a sudden downpour of rain, and their implications if you ignore them. Being aware of how the car is behaving is critical not only to where you finish in the race, but whether you finish at all. For instance, it would be stupid to keep racing at full pace if you are unable to see cars in front or behind, your final position is assured and there are only a couple of laps remaining. Instead, it is better to throttle back very slightly, thus preserving your engine and tyres and lessening the chance of mechanical failure. Do not relax your concentration, though, as you should still be alert to the possibilities of someone catching you up, or a driver ahead slowing or making a mistake.

The ideal driving style throughout a race is to be relaxed but alert and to have settled into an even rhythm as soon as possible after the start. The odd fast lap will not help you very much to reel in the opposition, nor to build up the gap between you and following cars. It takes time, but the value of consistency cannot be underestimated.

The key race tactics you will need to deploy are covered in more detail in the next chapter so, for now, let us 'fast-forward' to the close of the race.

Finishing
Seeing the chequered flag waved as you cross the finishing line will cause mixed feelings, depending on your position in the race or class. As you cross the line you should ease off the throttle to begin the aptly-named 'slowing down' lap, but do still keep alert as accidents can – and do – still occur at this late stage, especially when other drivers relax their concentration.

If you have actually won, the details in your Final Instructions will have specified whether you should proceed round to the start line to receive your winner's garland before completing a victory lap, but for the rest of the competitors the same procedure as described for the end of the practice session must be followed, which means you will be waved into the exit lane and back into the paddock. Again, slow down to a safe speed and keep your helmet on until you finally come to a halt in the paddock.

There, as you climb out of the car, with adrenalin still coursing through your veins, if you ever held the view that racing is all about egos your suspicions are about to be realized with the reactions of your fellow competitors. Most drivers will fall into three categories: those who have done well and want to let everyone know about it; those who did not do so well, perhaps not even finishing, and who explain to anyone who will listen exactly why this was the case – this usually includes a number of problems with the clutch/engine/brakes, but never any reference to their driving ability – and finally, those who are content no matter where they have finished (at least that is what they will tell you!).

Post-race debrief

It may be a drag, but if you hope to maintain your performance, or to improve it for the next race, it is essential that you assess just what happened from start to finish, and this is best achieved when the event is still fresh in your memory. As time elapses from the end of your race so the mind conveniently tends to overlook the car's under-performance and the driver's shortcomings. It is impossible to achieve any degree of impartiality or opinion based on comparative performance from the driver's seat, so the observations of a friend are invaluable in this respect. A debrief, complete with written notes, will be extremely helpful when the details of the event begin to be blurred at the edges, which is usually within a few hours.

You may think you had a good race, but this will only be borne out by two facts: your final position and your lap times.

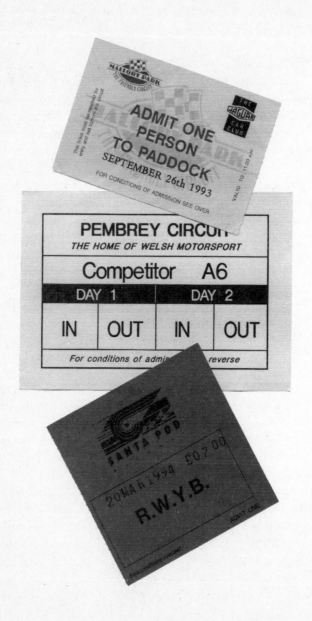

CHAPTER 9

Racecraft

"Understeer is when you go into a bank nose-first. Oversteer is when you hit the bank with the back-end first."
Tony Lanfranchi

You cannot rely solely on a book to teach you how to be a good race driver: this can only be achieved through practical experience on the track. Hopefully, though, this chapter will at least provide some useful tips and help you to focus on some of the key aspects associated with driving quickly and in safety, collectively described here as 'racecraft'.

The acquisition of this knowledge is traditionally based on entering races and then being subjected to a steep learning curve making expensive, time-consuming and potentially life-threatening mistakes as you progress. We have all been – or subsequently seen – a nervous novice pacing up and down, ashen-faced, in the assembly area, yet the first race need not be a triumph of luck over catastrophe. As touched on with regard to testing sessions, if racecraft is recognized as being as important as car preparation and drivers spend a little time on fine-tuning their own abilities as well as the car's, faster and safer lap times will result.

A comparable situation is that most people can jog and a few may even excel over a distance if they are fit, but there is a huge difference between them being able to run in competition. Take this a stage further, and as the field of runners becomes more competitive the athlete must concentrate on technique, consistency and tactics and rely on the advice and guidance of a good coach. Yet the use of tuition is greatly undervalued in motorsport, perhaps because of financial constraints, but probably more so by ego. Most drivers on the road think themselves amongst the elite, so the chances of a racing driver admitting that he would benefit from the advice of someone else is fairly remote.

If your pride allows, though, a few hours spent under the critical eye of an experienced and observant race driving instructor will pay dividends on the track and help to identify any failings in your driving style that can then hopefully be rectified. If bad habits can be caught at an early stage and you learn the basics, it will help to build a better foundation for your own individual style of driving without any wasted effort and help to identify the cause of time being lost on the track.

Remember, too, that tuition is not just for the novice, but is worth considering even if you are already an accomplished racer as it is never too late to learn more. After a winter of working on the car, why not treat yourself to a refresher course? It is surprising how quickly your confidence can fade and your technique become 'rusty'.

If you are convinced by these arguments, your best course of action is to telephone a convenient circuit and ask to speak to one of their senior instructors. If you then explain a few details of what you will be racing and the type of coaching you require, they should be able to tailor some instruction to your needs at a reasonable price, especially if you are prepared to attend for a session at lunchtime, when the school's business clientele are busy eating and regaling each other with tales of their exploits.

Whilst on this subject, do not bother with any of the standard half-day or one-day courses that are geared-up to provide corporate entertainment or are given as surprise birthday presents as these will be too superficial; visit some circuits these days and you begin to wonder how they ever manage to fit motor racing into their intensive schedule!

Before you can expect to drive with any degree of confidence on a track there are a number of basic principles that need to be mastered. First, you must be able to recognize the correct lines through corners, when to brake, and so forth, and only then are you realistically able to apply that knowledge in competition with other drivers. Racing is not just about driving fast, it is also about competing, and the two require different, but complementary skills that need to be practised and co-ordinated. First the basic driving techniques will be considered, then their application on the track.

Back to basics
Your experience of driving on the road may well have made you a safe driver, but from a racing perspective is also likely to have instilled you with all manner of bad habits picked up through a combination of laziness, boredom and the predictability of modern driving. When you are hard-pressed for time or encounter an open country road you may drive quicker than normal and think yourself 'a good driver', but in reality you are probably fooling yourself and your shortfalls will swiftly be shown up on a race track.

As an example, I never realized until quite late that I

'slipped the wheel' when cornering – a common practice on the road, but a cardinal sin when racing. The situation was admittedly not helped by my driving position in the car, but I am not using this as an excuse: I should have realized and taken positive action. One of the problems is that the normal driving position in a saloon car does not lend itself easily to a racing style of steering, as if the wheel is at the right place and you can touch the pedals you usually find the gear-lever is out of reach, or vice versa. (The best compromise is to try to reduce the length of the steering column and drop it slightly, taking care to ensure that there is adequate clearance.)

With your hands on either side of the wheel you will find that not only can you steer more easily, but you will feel more through the wheel – and your reactions to any necessary steering correction will be considerably quicker. It is possible to cross your arms marginally if the corner is tight, but as this will probably necessitate a slow speed anyway it should not pose any problem. In reality you will probably find that the only time you will need to reposition your hands is on tight hairpins.

The other advantage in having your arms in a constant position on the steering wheel is that should the car begin to slide uncontrollably, at least you know which way the wheels are pointing when the car eventually comes to a halt or slows sufficiently to become under control again. Once you are able to steer with confidence, many of the other techniques will flow naturally.

The way that you drive will also be affected by whether you are driving a front-wheel-drive or rear-wheel-drive car. There follows a brief examination of the two different styles of driving that each demands.

Front-wheel drive
My first experience of a front-wheel-drive car was my father

joyously tearing a Talbot Horizon, of all things, around our block, and very impressive it was as well. At each corner he urged me to admire the fact that all you needed to do was point the front of the car and accelerate. If I had not been concentrating on bracing my feet on the glovebox and had kept my eyes open I might have seen one of the safer road characteristics of FWD cars in that if you drive too fast they understeer to the extent that they will always go straight on rather than spin with potentially lethal consequences.

On a race car this attribute is wholly undesirable, however, as it does not allow the car to be driven quicker than the in-built understeer will allow. The frustration of trying to drive a car quickly that basically wants to carry straight on at every corner cannot be imagined – you need to have experienced it for yourself. It is rather like trying to manoeuvre a heavy shopping trolley around the end of the aisle at speed.

Generally, however, just as understeer can be predicted, it can also be physically limited through modifying the car's suspension and by adopting a particular driving style. It perhaps goes without saying that as the driven wheels are also used to steer the car, grip is critical and the performance abilities of the tyres and the inter-action between bodyroll and spring/damper arrangements are the key areas on which to concentrate when setting up the car.

Naturally, this must be finely balanced or the car will exhibit oversteer and therefore negate the advantage of neutral handling. You should also note that the car may now enter and travel through corners very well, but be less easy to steer when exiting corners or in a straight line. Another frustrating element is that of the car's front end tending to lift as it exits a corner, thus reducing traction to the driving wheels.

If understeer is experienced the temptation is to apply more power to bring the back around, but if this does not happen the understeer will only become worse. The extreme options of taking your foot completely off the accelerator or braking mid-corner will usually result in the car spinning, so the answer, tiresome though it may seem, is to 'bleed off' the excess speed gradually (by *gently* easing off the accelerator – not by braking!) and incrementally turning out more with the steering wheel until the front wheels grip. You cannot fight understeer.

Rear-wheel drive
With all the problems of front-wheel drive outlined above it is not surprising that many drivers prefer to race a rear-wheel-drive car – not least through tradition. One of the main advantages of driving such a car is that it not only behaves more responsively, but in the right hands can be steered using the accelerator as well as the steering wheel. Back off the power and the front end will back off the corner whilst more power will cause the back end to swing out.

This is not to say that it does not suffer any vices, however. If you brake too early in a RWD car it will exhibit the same tendency to understeer as its FWD counterpart; although the ability to control steering through judicious use of power is superb when it is balanced correctly, too much power will result in oversteer.

This interplay between application of brakes, power and steering is one that needs to be practised to ensure that the optimum speed through corners is reached. Despite the ability to steer on the accelerator it is important to remember that the front wheels are also useful in this regard! Power-drifting a car through a corner only to find the front wheels are at odds on the exit is commonplace, and results in crossed arms and panic in the cockpit as the car veers violently when the front tyres grip.

Cornering

All corners, whether fast or slow, consist of three elements: approach, apex and exit – and all are interlinked.

Surprisingly, the correct line to any corner is the same whatever your speed, so it is worth getting this aspect right before you decide to attack it so quickly that you cannot control the car if it all goes wrong.

Your focus in all corners should not be trying to get around them quickly, but to exit them at as high a speed as possible – which is a different concept entirely. Cornering with all four tyres screeching may look dramatic for the spectators, but in reality all you are doing is scrubbing off speed and expensive rubber.

Finally, throughout all cornering your movements should be gradual and precise to avoid unnecessary strain on the car and driver as generally the smoother your actions the faster the car will be.

The approach

'Slow in – fast out' has long been a maxim used in racing to describe the way a corner should be tackled, and it still holds true today. It requires careful judgment to gauge initially the optimum turning-in point and then the speed at which the corner can be taken, but the ideal is to have the car exiting at the maximum possible speed. Once this decision has been made the car can be slowed through easing off the throttle in the case of slow corners or braking should speed need to be reduced further. The speed of entry will also have a marked effect on the stability of the car: your suspension should be set up to the optimum forces and movements it is subjected to through the corner, so being too slow could be as unsettling as being too fast.

Ideally, all braking should be carried out in a straight line up to the point of turning into the corner, but as late as possible, without locking up the wheels or being unable to

RACING TECHNIQUE: ONE

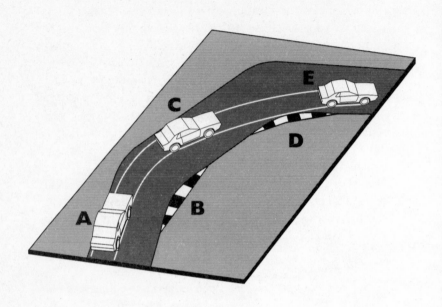

DOUBLE APEX

A	*Braking to a reasonable speed*
B	*Ignore first apex*
C	*Turning to second apex*
D	*Clip apex - power on*
E	*Allow car to drift*

RACING TECHNIQUE: TWO

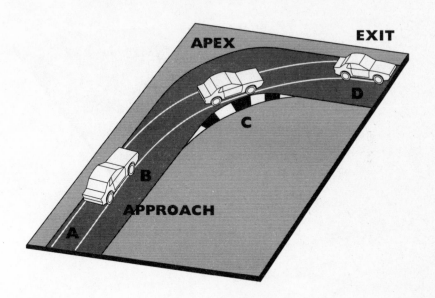

OPTIMUM RACING LINE

A Braking to a reasonable speed

B Off brakes - turning

C Apex of bend - power on

D Allow car to drift

RACING TECHNIQUE: THREE

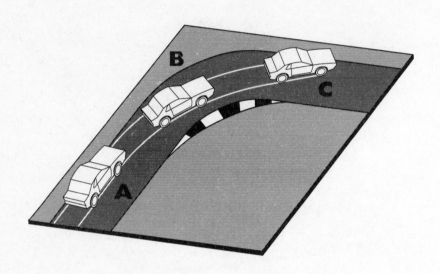

UNDERSTEER

A   *Car approaches too fast*

B   *Driver turns in but car does not respond*

C   *Car fails to turn and continues straight on*

RACING TECHNIQUE: FOUR

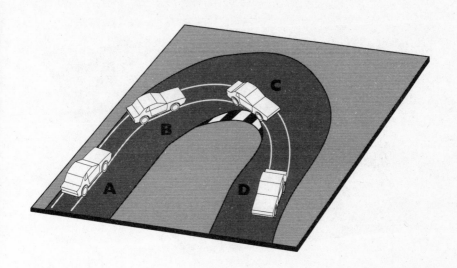

HAIRPIN

A	*Braking to a reasonable speed*
B	*Turn into apex*
C	*Clip apex - power on*
D	*Allow car to drift*

RACING TECHNIQUE: FIVE

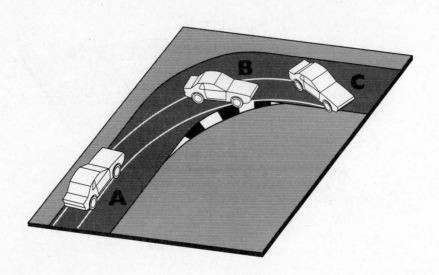

OVERSTEER

A   *Car approaches too fast
or turns in on a trailing brake.*

B   *Back end of car steps out - too fast /
power too early (correction is to steer
to left / lift off power).*

C   *Correction fails as speed is too fast.*

RACING TECHNIQUE: SIX

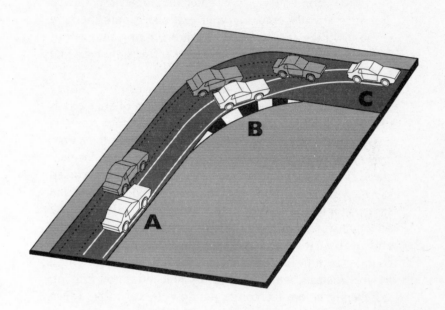

LATE BRAKING

A   Driver take the wide line to the approaching corner.

B   Driver brakes marginally later and allows car to drift slightly wide of corner.

C   Car allowed to drift and takes up position ahead of other competitor.

slow sufficiently in time. This will mean that the car is travelling as fast as possible for the longest possible period of time, which means that less time will have been taken. Brake too soon and you will enter the corner too slowly, thus dramatically reducing your exit speed onto the next straight. Brake too late and you are running the risk of losing control of the car and spinning off or sliding on and bowing out of the race.

Due to technological improvements in tyres, mainly through greater tyre-wall rigidity and the use of compounds offering more grip, braking during the corner itself is possible and indeed may be necessary if you take the corner either too fast or off-line, or you need to slow for an incident ahead. Wherever possible, however, this should be avoided as you will already be finely balancing speed, adhesion and steering into the corner and any braking will shift the effective weight of the car, causing it to become unstable and probably spin. It can be done with practice and confidence in the car's behaviour, but it is inadvisable for a novice. Instead, it is far better to concentrate on braking sufficiently before the corner to allow the car to be driven around at maximum speed.

One of the dangers in all high-speed approaches is that of leaving the braking so late that you lose control of the car, or being tempted to keep the brakes applied through the opening section of the corner itself as you turn in (this is known as a 'trailing brake'). Although it may seem natural to try to bleed-off speed in this way and virtually be an uncontrolled reflex, it is also making the car unstable, so again it should be avoided.

Much will depend on your car's braking capabilities, but as a rule all braking should be firm yet progressive as a stamping action may not only lock up the wheels, but also cause the car to become unbalanced. If your wheels lock up, yet you still need to slow the car, lift your foot from the brake pedal and then brake again, but in successive short bursts. Known as 'cadence braking', this technique means that the wheels will be braked yet still be allowed to turn and thus prevent skidding.

Once slowed, a lower gear suitable for accelerating out of the corner needs to be selected before you turn in.

Apex

The apex is the point of the corner closest to the car as it turns in, yet it is not necessarily the midpoint as its position depends on the width of the available track and the corner angle. After turning in, you should let the car settle into the corner and be aiming to clip the apex. As the car does so, the power can be reapplied firmly but smoothly – accelerate too early and you will go wide, miss the apex and lose time.

On wide sweeping corners, such as Gerard's at Mallory Park, Coram Curve at Snetterton and, to a degree, the revised Copse at Silverstone, the power is applied virtually throughout as the clipping point is so early. Here, the ideal situation is to have the car set up on a knife-edge and drifting on as much power as you dare. The technique is nerve-wracking and emphasizes again the need for you to be aware of your car's capabilities (which in turn will lead to you knowing your own).

For more acute bends, however, such as Shaw's at Mallory Park and Russell at Snetterton, the clipping point is later, so the power is applied later.

Exit

If you approach a corner at the correct point and speed you should clip the apex and exit at the highest possible speed and at the right attitude. Get the approach wrong, however, through being off-line, steering too little/much or at too high/low a speed, and you will either at best exit slower than the optimum, or at worst lose control, with potentially damaging consequences.

As the approach will effectively determine the exit, there should be little adjustment necessary, but the car should be allowed to drift wide under progressive acceleration. At the exit point it is tempting to bring the car back on line for the next corner too early, but as this will only increase the side loading on the tyres and reduce speed, you should use all of the track that is needed.

Whilst such principles are all very clean, measured and appear easy on paper, in reality they take some time to become second nature, and it may even take quite a few seasons to master a really awkward corner properly. In competition the problem is understandably worse as the ideal line into every corner is the one that all drivers want to take. You may find yourself blocked or off-line, so you should be prepared to take a different line into a corner and, as already mentioned, exercise caution if using the dirty parts of the track off the racing line as they will offer less grip.

Rhythm
Do you ever remember playing with a Scalextric set, 'blipping' the handset on as you exited a corner, then pulling off the power at the next bend? Eventually, if the circuit was small and repetitive your hand movements controlling the speed became automatic, coincidental to the position of the car on the track, and you settled into a rhythm. That same repetitive action, when transferred to a proper race track, is better known as consistency and is one of the key attributes to being a better race driver. It is no good being superbly quick for one lap and then many seconds slower the next and unable to recognize why. Instead, it is necessary to be able to lap at an even speed, yet know or anticipate where small fractions of time can be saved and then gradually cause the lap times to fall. This is

difficult if you are on a strange circuit in a short race, but proves the importance of the practice session earlier in the day.

Straights

Most circuits have at least one long straight where you can relax for a few seconds and take stock of your situation. This does not mean you should take a break, though, as the time should be used to check your instruments and above all to think: think of how many laps you have left; whether you are taking a certain corner incorrectly and why; can you keep on the power for longer and brake later on this next lap?; where are the opposition and are they gaining on you?

The main straight is usually adjacent to the pit area, and from the pit wall you will receive messages as to how you are progressing. You should be hoping for constant or, ideally, falling lap times as the race progresses.

Straights, if long enough, also offer the opportunity to use another competitor's speed to your advantage by slipstreaming. The technique is to exit the corner as close as possible to the car in front and to keep tucked in behind it as you both accelerate. With the leading car taking the full force of air resistance, your engine should be operating at lower rpm to achieve the same speed as the other car and, depending on the length of the straight, you should be able to pull out and still have a reserve of power which, in theory, can be used to overtake. This will not work if you try to overtake too early as the effect will not have accrued to your advantage and, in fact, may work against you if you are not sufficiently close to the car ahead and have to negotiate the turbulent air in its wake.

Avoidance tactics, if you are about to fall prey to being slipstreamed, are to ensure that the following car is kept as remote or off-line from you as possible. However, excess weaving will be treated fairly harshly by observers and consequently the Clerk of the Course – who generally will be well placed to view the proceedings anyway – so keep such manoeuvres within reason. It is just as effective to accelerate as quickly as possible from the corner preceding the straight and keep to the natural racing line into the next corner, leaving the feint move and clever undertaking manoeuvre until proficiency allows.

Slipstreaming is only really practical on long straights and in races where the cars are running at high speeds, when the proportional advantage in the speed differential is greater. However, even if slipstreaming is not practically possible as an intimidatory tactic, looming large in someone's mirrors a few inches from them with a corner fast approaching certainly has its merits.

Overtaking

Overtaking another car on a racetrack for the first time is one of life's great moments, even if the car in question is limping back to the pits! The temptation for you to 'blow its doors off' – or other such racing parlance – is legitimate if the slower car is on the racing line, but deliberate swerving or cutting up will not impress the course officials if deemed to be unnecessary and in fact dangerous.

Apart from showing a little courtesy for the other driver, it also makes sense to give slower cars a wide berth for your own sake as they may be leaking oil or suffering from a mechanical failure that could cause them to be extremely unpredictable in your path. If they carry a novice cross, indicating that this is likely to be their first season, you may also like to cast your mind back to your own initial experiences on a circuit and the lack of respect you felt for your fellow competitors when it happened to you.

In the case of a car considerably slower than your own, your main concern should be to make sure that the driver in front is aware of your presence and that you can overtake as cleanly and swiftly as possible. This is especially advantageous if it leaves the slower car sandwiched between you and an opponent with a corner approaching, as it will delay them and allow you to press on. As you get nearer to the backmarker, you should therefore look out for any hand signals. An alert and courteous slower driver will wave you through on the inside, whereas if you creep up unannounced they will not have the chance to give you this advantage. If your relative speeds are quite large it does not do any harm to switch on your lights, especially if you are one of the first few cars to begin to lap backmarkers – who may not be expecting you – or the cars you are approaching are caught up in a private race of their own.

Naturally, not every car you approach will be so slow and subservient; circuit racing would be a fairly one-sided leisure pursuit if they were. The experience of battling it out with another driver *is* racing, and one of the main reasons for being there. To be at the front of the race or your class is the ultimate position, but equally enjoyable is the thrill of dicing with a like-minded competitor in a car of equal performance. There is something far more satisfying in racing flat-out for 10 laps than touring round on your own for the same distance on a clear track and finishing marginally higher up the field.

The typical battle for position will involve you pitting your wits against another driver of equal ability and machinery – so what will determine who crosses the line first? The key in any form of conflict, whether it be motor racing, chess or fencing, involves exploiting weaknesses in your opponent so, if equally matched, in the early stages it will pay you to observe rather than just make a rash move at the first opportunity. That said, if you approach unannounced and can make a clear overtaking manoeuvre, then do it. Too often it is impossible to gather and use that initial approaching momentum to the best effect, and although you may be quicker you cannot 'will' yourself past.

Apart from the clean overtaking manoeuvre on the straight, through the use of more power or being able to apply it earlier, the available places for overtaking are largely limited to the approaches to corners through out-braking or better positioning. Following your rival through a series of corners will enable you to assess his braking points – are they too early? Is he taking the car in too shallow or too deeply? Where is the best place to pounce? Also, this shadowing, especially at close quarters, has the added advantage of applying pressure on your opponent, who perhaps will begin to make mistakes which you should be ready to exploit.

If your opponent is experienced, he will not surrender his position easily and will try his utmost to prevent you passing. This can involve blocking the line to the corners – preventing you from taking the inner line under braking – or driving you out wide (if you try to overtake on the outside).

The counter to such tactics is to feint your moves and try to catch out your opponent by making a move that is unexpected or is so positive that it cannot be challenged. Commitment when overtaking needs to be absolute, yet not suicidal, and positive to the extent of being inevitable rather a preamble to a 50/50 pile-up.

Blocking tactics by your opponent are acceptable providing none of the actions could be deemed as dangerous and intended to cause you to come to grief. In the heat of the race, driving wheel-to-wheel for five or six laps is exhilarating and, if fair, justifies more than all of the time and effort you have expended. On the other hand, being baulked, blocked and barged is too much like hard work both at the time and afterwards, when having to repair the damage. In such a situation it is difficult to advise anything but restraint because retaliation will normally provide no solution. You may believe you are the only two racers on the track, but following cars may well add weight to the observations of marshals and other officials who will have observed you both throughout the race.

The rules regarding overtaking are clear in that the car which has its front wheels level with or ahead of the other driver's seated position is judged to have the right of way into the approaching corner. This sounds simple, but in a pack of cars each trying to out-brake the other the small print can easily be forgotten. It is sometimes very difficult to distinguish between bloody-mindedness, panic, driver error and malice, but in all instances try to keep cool and be patient.

If you genuinely believe a competitor has acted unfairly, then use the correct channels and lodge an objection rather than whinge about it afterwards. Those drivers who follow the maxim: "Put up or shut up", may encounter unpopularity, but they will also earn respect.

Defending your position

The rules that govern claiming priority on the approach to a corner are fine in theory, but they presume that the other driver has seen you and is still looking (which both have subtle nuances). In reality, in order to defend your position effectively you must prevent any opponent from drawing alongside on the inside line of any approaching corner and, if possible, prevent them from overtaking you through pure speed differential on the straights by breaking any slipstreaming advantage.

Defending on corners is much easier than it sounds if you keep calm, use your mirrors – carefully – and position the car correctly. Panic can easily set in if the other driver uses intimidatory tactics such as getting close to your rear bumper, looming at either side of you, and beginning to test your nerve by trying to outbrake you into some of the corners. One of the best ways of avoiding such tactics being effective is to keep your eyes fixed to the track ahead and on the racing line of the approaching corners. This will at least ensure that your car is correctly set up, whilst keeping your opponent in your peripheral vision will allow you to know his position without allowing him to dominate your driving. It is important that you drive your own race: lost concentration through watching the car behind (driving on your mirrors) will lead to you missing a turning or braking point, which will be exploited fully by others.

Tight and twisty circuits, where overtaking points are limited, lend themselves well to blocking tactics through careful use of braking at the approaches to each corner. Over-braking, for want of a better word, will have the effect of slowing you down, but will frustrate your following opponent, who will be unable to overtake if you keep to the racing line and accelerate quickly out of each corner. Over-braking will also unsettle the following driver by breaking up his natural rhythm and perhaps even allowing other cars to catch him up and start to contend his position – which is a welcome distraction as far as you are concerned.

In such situations it is not uncommon for such frustration to lead to a few friendly taps on the rear of the car and 'do-or-die' efforts in the closing stages of the race. So be prepared, keep calm and stay on the racing line.

Being overtaken

Whilst such a prospect may abhor you, it does happen if there are cars much quicker than you on the circuit, so it is best covered. There appear to be two trains of thought about being overtaken: resist it at all costs and keep to the racing line come what may; or acquiesce to faster cars and let them pass. There is no definitive answer to this dilemma, as much actually depends on the relative speeds of the two or more cars involved.

Do not presume that I am implying you will be trailing

around at the back of the field. There may be times when you will be in a combined race where, due to a small entry, the organizers have merged you with much faster cars. If you are a backmarker, impeding the fast-approaching leading pack through bloody-mindedness is stupid and will not win you any friends but, on the other hand, blocking a car that has virtually the same performance as yours is fair game.

Later, as you gain more experience, you will be skilled enough, if being lapped, to move off the racing line and allow the leaders through. However, if you are a novice you are better off in your first races by being predictable and keeping to the racing line, not making any sudden changes in direction; let the faster drivers use their speed and greater experience to find the best way around you. This will also prevent you falling into the trap of benevolently moving out of the way for the leader, only to have the unnoticed but closely following driver of the second-placed car being forced to swerve to take avoiding action or, at worst, actually hitting you.

As one can imagine, the need to use your mirrors on the track cannot be emphasized enough, although to see some drivers, oblivious to anything behind them, you could be forgiven for thinking them to be mere decoration. Again, make sure you adjust your mirrors every time you go out on the track to suit your driving position when strapped in, that you eliminate any blindspots and, most important of all, that you remember to use them!

Taking risks

During a race you will face many risks, but those involving a degree of choice should be determined by a calculated decision, and instinct based on experience rather than sudden impulse or retribution. The ability to make cool decisions under pressure is something attributed to great or gifted drivers, but is usually more to do with having a positive state of mind. This is not just something that happens, but is part of a learning process that can take years, but after a few seasons at least you should be aware of the vagaries of 'track logic' that will befall you. Examples – and there are many – are that races are not won at the first corner, that the unanticipated is more probable, and that you will never know everything; thinking that you are finally ahead of the game is usually the precursor to something going wrong!

On a more serious note, when taking risks on the track it is incumbent on you to think not only of the risk to yourself and your car, but also the implications of your actions on other competitors. Enough said.

Accident avoidance

Many drivers, unfortunate enough to have been involved in an accident, and assuming they saw what hit them, will sometimes describe the event as having happened in 'slow motion', whereas from an external observer's viewpoint, it will probably have only taken a matter of seconds. This marked difference in perception is largely due to the driver being so keenly alert to the environment, absorbing information and having to make decisions in minute fractions of time; everything is happening pretty fast out there and time can play tricks on you very easily.

The loss of grip at the rear of the car, for example, is registered as it occurs and is corrected instantly. Similarly, when loss of adhesion causes the car to spin, the amount of information being fed to the brain combined with thoughts of what can be done to avoid hitting another car, frustration and pure fear, result in time appearing to drag. Meanwhile, as the rear of the car steps out and the Armco barrier looms closer, time appears to slow, you are unable to respond and instead seem frozen, like a rabbit caught in the lights of an oncoming car.

Accidents do not just happen – they are caused – and so, extending such logic, they can be avoided with a little care. All accidents, bar acts of God, can be divided into two distinct categories: mechanical failure and driver error. The former could be due to poor car preparation or a component being overstressed, ready examples including a puncture, a split brake pipe or a jammed throttle. In all cases it is important to note that the risk of these occurring could be limited by preventative maintenance.

Driver error, which could in fact include a combination of drivers' errors, is the most common reason for accidents, however, although few drivers would admit it. Again, these could be avoided if the same preparedness lavished on the car were extended to the driver.

Within this latter category are problems associated with braking far too late, cornering at too high a speed, and so forth. In fact, to be honest, all the areas of risk are part of what makes the sport so enjoyable. Test pilots have a phrase "pushing the envelope", which describes how they test a plane to its outer limits of stability, and to a certain degree you too should be able do this on a race track, albeit two-dimensionally, in safety. It is unfortunate that it is often beyond the competence of some drivers to know when they are out of their depth and making the wrong decision. As already mentioned, to drive at the limit you need to know what those limits are. It is far better to back off in an impending mass pile-up – and perhaps take advantage of it – rather than be the owner of one of those sorry cars that gets towed in when the race has finished. Looking ahead on a race track is as valid as it is on a motorway.

If you are unfortunate enough to be involved in an accident there are a number of split decisions that you will need to make, depending on your predicament:

• If the car cannot be driven, yet still lies on the track, obey the marshals who will advise you. Do not get out of the car unless instructed.

• If the car is drivable, yet cannot continue in the race, drive it into the nearest position of safety off-track.

• Before leaving the car, isolate the electrics.

These scenarios presume that you have been in a minor collision or 'encounter with the scenery', but there may be an occasion when the situation is far more serious, the possibility of fire being the most feared, yet happily infrequent occurrence.

If you experience an on-board fire whilst driving, do not stop abruptly and leave the car unless it is immediately life-threatening (I will leave such a definition to your discretion!). Instead, it is far safer for you to drive/coast the car to the nearest marshal's post where skilled and equipped marshals will be able to deal with the problem more quickly and easily, with less risk to yourself and the chance of less damage to the car.

Obviously, if the fire is extreme you may need to take immediate action yourself. In such an instance, slow down the car, and keep off the racing line before tackling the fire through activating an automatic system. Then pull the car off the circuit completely before you try to put it out with a hand-held extinguisher. Remember also to isolate the electrics – which may have contributed to the fire occurring initially.

Driving in the wet
Not all of your racing will be under perfect blue skies. At the start of the season, in particular, you are likely to encounter a wide range of conditions from snow and hail to gales. Driving in the wet is a great equalizer as it reduces the advantage of cars that have more power, and it places a greater emphasis on driving ability. First, though, to get the best out of the car, wherever possible you should adjust its

suspension settings to suit the prevailing conditions. In order to ensure more compliance and grip, anti-roll bar settings should be slackened off and dampers should be set to soft. Wet-weather tyres should be fitted and their pressures should also be reduced.

Other wet-weather preparations that may be overlooked by competitors include:

• Spraying the under-bonnet electrics with a water inhibitor such as WD40.

• Methodically cleaning the glass areas and perhaps applying a rain repellant such as Rainex to the outside and an anti-misting gel to the inside of the front windscreen as mentioned earlier.

• Testing that the windscreen wipers are in good order and that they work and the washer bottle is topped up. As a scrutineer once stated: "You can be driving an Aston Martin and be the slowest car on the circuit if you can't see where you are going."

• Checking that the windscreen demister works effectively. Even so, it is prudent to have a small leather in the car.

• Checking that the car is waterproof. If water enters the car it will usually cause the windows to steam up quickly.

Driving in the wet requires sensitivity at the controls as any dramatic steering, acceleration or braking is punished. Nevertheless, you are still racing, so need to drive at the limits that the conditions will allow, which is best achieved through gradual progression and testing. Step the back end out and get it to come back, try to push the car to the limit of its braking and attempt cadence braking as described earlier. This testing is needed so that you are aware of the limits to which you can drive.

If you are in a wet practice session you should start slowly and build up speed, gradually getting used to the way that the car behaves. Yet if practice was dry and the weather has subsequently changed for the worst prior to the race, you must try to achieve this learning process in the warm-up laps.

Off the grid you will encounter more wheelspin, so be a little easier on the clutch and change up to second gear as soon as possible. As adhesion will be poor you should also expect other cars to snake sideways as they fight for grip.

Around the circuit, your vision will be impaired by rain and spray kicked up by the cars, so it may be necessary to drive slightly off-line, especially when overtaking, in order to see ahead. Also, remember that such poor vision extends behind you as well, so check your mirrors carefully and use your lights.

CHAPTER 10

Sponsorship
– a personal
account

"Sponsorship is the hardest part for everyone."
Robin Knox-Johnston
The Times, January 12, 1989

It is estimated that the total amount of money spent annually
on sports sponsorship in the UK rose from £129 million in
1985 to £226 million in 1990 (*Henley Centre for
Forecasting 1990: The economic impact of sport in the UK*).
Although such figures are impressive, it is also worth noting
that this was only 10 per cent of that spent on advertising in
the press or on television for the same period.

So, although initially the amounts being spent on
sponsorship may appear large, they are still dwarfed in
comparison with the budgets dedicated to conventional
media, and not without good reason. A business, when
placing any sort of advertisement, is largely entering
familiar territory and is able to analyze the market for its
goods or services, target a particular audience by their

lifestyle and deliver an appropriate message. It is this ability to define and subsequently monitor the impact of advertising that makes it attractive: it is established, tested and it works.

Sponsorship, however, is a less precise medium that tends to help maintain a company's profile over a period of time rather than offer short-term coverage. On the outer fringe of advertising, it probably has more in common with patronage, but nevertheless, it is still a valuable business tool. Used correctly with forethought and preparation by both parties, it can satisfy both the aspirations of the sponsor and sponsored and be a mutually beneficial partnership.

So, what makes a business decide to sponsor? Basically, there are three key reasons, and you should bear these in mind when you are trying to attract sponsorship at whatever level:

To stimulate awareness A household name only becomes so by extensive advertising, and sponsorship is a key aspect of this. Many companies also have a need to raise their profile within a specialist marketplace, even if they have no direct dealings with the public. Certain sponsorship activities in a close market can be a tremendous boost to a company's profile and achieve the worthwhile side-effect of having a dispiriting effect on the company's competitors, sending a clear message to them that "we are still around and doing well".

To entertain clients or customers Corporate entertainment is still a successful and enjoyable way of mixing business and pleasure, and motorsport is an attractive spectacle that will appeal to many, even at a fairly elementary level. Even a local low-key sprint championship is an event that can be interesting providing it is packaged honestly and you find the right sponsor. The ability to look behind the scenes at a race meeting is a unique opportunity for a sponsor and guests, especially when they can associate with a participant and feel as if they are part of the action.

To engender goodwill To some the ideal sponsorship deal is one where the sponsor's motives are philanthropic, but there are usually other influences that are more commercial. In reality, being a sponsor has rewards that cannot be defined in financial terms, such as an improved image, for instance. Sponsorship does, after all, tend to elevate the esteem of the company, whether it is from simply involving the staff to projecting a benevolent attitude.

As you can imagine, the range of sports available to a potential sponsor is very wide, with different types being favoured according to the image of the company. You therefore can expect an insurance agency or bank to sponsor cricket, golf or tennis whereas generally they will steer clear of sports where the image is less in keeping with theirs, such as darts or bungee-jumping, for instance. This fact will at least help to steer you towards those businesses with a more dynamic image who may be more likely to support activities such as motorsport. Do not forget, though, that there may also be companies who will want to change their image or attract a younger clientele.

Whilst narrowing down the type of prospective sponsors may marginally improve your chances of success, never forget that it is a buyer's market, so you should also ask yourself what makes you so special from the rest? Your chances are small, as the following description of my early attempts will prove.

Before this, I have to admit that although I have given an honest version of events as they occurred I have played down the frustration and low points to a degree to stop you becoming too depressed. If, as a result, it all appears too easy, this was not the case in reality. The lessons learnt are practical, personal and hence non-exhaustive, but I hope you will be able to apply them to your own situation and improve your chances of finding support through perseverance and innovation.

First season

In preparation for my first season of racing, I foolishly believed that most major companies with an involvement in motorsport would be certain to beat a path to my garage door, bearing lucrative sponsorship deals based on the available area of car body panels. I did not even think of trying to improve my chances of finding a sponsor by perhaps researching the subject or even trying to work out a strategy.

Nonchalantly, I drew up a list of potential sponsors by trawling through a large pile of motoring magazines and assessed each of the advertisements in turn. By the end of the hour I had a 'wish list' of some of the most powerful and influential sponsors in motorsport – what could be easier? Before the day was out I had whittled down the list and sent out approximately 20 mailshots. Each of these consisted of a laser colour photocopy of the car, together with a covering letter. This described the championship I wished to contend, listed the dates and venues for the year ahead and concluded by unashamedly asking for financial support in the form of money or discounts.

As you can imagine, the majority of companies did not even bother to reply and those which did politely informed me, through a standard, mass-copied letter, that their budgets for the year had already been allocated. I actually doubt whether many of the mailshots even reached anyone in a position of influence as I did not mark the envelopes for any one person's particular attention, relying instead on the company themselves to direct it straight to the top. Among those companies that did reply, I received a letter from a Rover dealer which seemed to sum up the problems I was facing, wittily stating that "due to economic understeer and chequered sales, unfortunately they could not support my racing campaign". They did, however, advise that I should not give up hope, which I never did.

Now, with the benefit of hindsight, I realize that although the recession was certainly an important factor and was to be quoted back at me on numerous occasions, it was not the sole dissuading influence and that essentially my approach had not been given sufficient thought. Nevertheless, I continued with this random mailshot technique and, despite it being blunt and primitive, actually managed to attract some small discounts from motoring and racing accessory shops, which at least was a start. Gradually, however, as responses became rarer I was forced to take stock of the situation and assess where I was going wrong. Even then, it was some time before it finally dawned on me that I was one of many club racers trying to chase scarce resources and that my likelihood of any substantial success was extremely remote.

It is obvious that those large and prominent companies that can afford to advertise extensively through national newspapers, television and radio are doing so to a carefully pre-planned strategy that suits their aims and objectives. Therefore, even if I had had a worthwhile proposal to offer them, it would have been too late for it to be considered alongside campaigns to which they were already committed. Also, it was most likely that I would be considered too small to warrant attention, and that therefore I represented an unjustifiable risk. All companies have to consider their image and so need to be sure that their name is associated with a proven product that can be trusted.

Eventually I reached the conclusion that well-known drivers with a proven track record, racing well-prepared cars in established series with media coverage, were far more likely to attract sponsorship than a novice. The only surprise was that it had taken me so long to realize this fact.

If that was not enough, another problem was that the championship in which I intended to take part was still in its infancy and not very exciting. Like many single-make series aimed at club level, it consisted of near-standard saloon cars with little or no modifications allowed in order to keep costs to a minimum. The result, whilst exhilarating from the driver's seat, was often very boring for spectators as speeds were slow and overtaking very rare; in the early days of the series it was often the most reliable car that would win, as long before the chequered flag fell the field of starters had been severely depleted. It seemed that more time was spent clearing up the smoking and broken cars littered around the circuit than on the actual race itself.

With not all of the registered cars competing at every event, grids were sometimes small, and it is no wonder that the overall championship leader at the end of the year had won, in effect, by attrition. These factors alone would have been enough to limit the appeal to any potential sponsors.

With the odds seemingly stacked against me, I decided to concentrate a little closer to home and began to speak to friends and work colleagues in the hope that they would be able to point me in the right direction. My employer at that time was fairly unsympathetic to requests for financial assistance – which was mainly due to the spectre of imminent bankruptcy, although I was unaware of this at the time – but business acquaintances were a little more interested in my venture and able to suggest various different avenues to explore, if not actually to provide any financial assistance.

It is through such contacts that I was able to emerge from my first season fairly low down the rankings, but with enough paint for a complete respray, courtesy of the

Autocolour Division of ICI. This 'support in kind' was an area of assistance that I had not even contemplated as until then I had been concentrating solely on raising money.

At this point, a useful partnership was also forged with the Rover Group who, like many of the main car dealers, offer discounted parts direct from their factory in Cowley through their Motorsport Division. Aside from the financial benefits of the scheme, it also ensures that your parts are 'genuine' rather than imported – and quite often sub-standard – reproduced items which could jeopardize your safety, particularly if they are key components when the car is being driven on the limit. In addition, the special tuning parts available from the factory also have the benefit of being tried and tested under vigorous conditions by works cars, so are a superlative option to standard parts.

In addition to discounted parts, Rover, like many other car manufacturers, also sponsor a number of race series featuring their latest models or engines and run an incentive scheme to reward winning drivers of current models in a variety of championships. To take advantage of the latter, all that is necessary is simply to register with them at the beginning of the season and carry discreet advertising on your car and racesuit.

Early lessons learnt
• Don't bother to write to major companies unless you have something substantially innovative to offer them – they will have heard it all before.
• Similarly, established companies that advertise in motor magazines are all regularly inundated with requests and you are likely to be disappointed by the lack of response.
• Do, however, write to companies who are new on the scene and may have a budget for advertising or sponsorship that may not yet be allocated.
• Consider mailshots carefully – too professional and lavish

an approach may be misread as not having your priorities correct and prompting the view that your limited money would have been better spent on the car. However, a badly prepared and scruffy mailshot will have a similar effect, but for the opposite reasons.

• Inquire through your local main dealer as to whether your car manufacturer has a support scheme for motorsport – this opportunity can also be used to seek some form of assistance from the dealer, if only for the loan of the occasional specialist tool that so many modern cars seem to require.

• Consider your personal contacts, but wisely: there is a fine line between asking for assistance and appearing to be begging or trying to exploit personal or business relationships. Remember that not everyone will share your enthusiasm.

• Lastly, once again, remember that obtaining any form of sponsorship in sport is difficult, and perhaps more so in motorsport where the competition is so fierce, so do not lose heart.

Second season

Whilst the car now looked like a million dollars, it also felt as if that was about the sum I needed to keep it going. Initially, enthusiasm had somewhat blinded me to the expense of my new-found pursuit, but now the true costs of being competitive were becoming apparent and I found myself in somewhat of a dilemma. In order to be competitive I needed to improve the car, and to do that cost money over and above the base budget that I required for race entry fees, licence cost, medical and so forth.

If I had been in any of the highly competitive single-seater series, this situation would have been exacerbated by my lack of competitiveness, thus turning away the interests of any potential sponsor. Such vicious circles are hard to break.

Again I reverted to the mailshot idea, but this time concentrated on medium-sized businesses in my area, hoping that the local connection would be an attraction, and even offering to make the car available for special promotion days. Aware of my previous mistakes, I also carried out some simple research over the telephone and at least discovered the name of the best person to whom I should write. If nothing else, this meant that it would be disregarded by someone whose job it was to do so!

The recession, however, had effectively ended my hope of a local benefactor, and my second season entered its closing stages with the car's engine temperature rising and my disposable income dropping to a low ebb. If I was to enjoy motorsport as a competitor rather than as a spectator, some form of financial assistance would need to be found very soon.

Clutching at straws, I even opened my local telephone directory and made an additional list of every company bearing the name 'Metro', as this was the model of car I was then driving. A shortlist was then made by omitting those whom I realized would not be in the slightest bit interested or were inappropriate, such as the local launderette! I was not to know at the time, but this name connection was eventually to lead to success, albeit from an unexpected angle.

I also tried a more sophisticated approach to the mailshots this time and made a simple line drawing of the car from a photograph and traced the company's masthead and logo onto the bonnet. With the addition of notes alongside, the idea was fairly effective and at least was more relevant than a simple letter and photograph.

In the meantime, I visited the Motor Racing Exhibition at Earls Court, mainly to collect more brochures and build up my list of prospective backers. As is so often the case in such stories, fate seemed to play its part as during a walk around I struck up a conversation with one of the exhibitors who was showing an MG Metro 6R4. Ben Parry kindly took an interest in my plight and invited me to call in and discuss the matter further. This I did the following week and after a tour of their facilities was offered unspecified rolling road time at a negotiable rate which turned out to be free, but invaluable.

I now realize that this was the turning point in my fortunes as it allowed me access to the luxuries of being able to have the engine tuned and developed to its optimum power within the class limitations rather than within mine. At last I would be able to compete on an equal footing. For this to happen, however, I would still need a main sponsor – and soon.

Third season
Just as I was beginning to come to terms with failure and the fact that I would probably not be racing the following season, yet another fortunate coincidence changed my circumstances for the better.

A manufacturer of heating appliances had written to me enclosing details of their new product range called Metro. So, with nothing to lose, I wrote to the Managing Director, thanking him for his letter, and asked whether they would consider using my car to promote their product further.

Harton Heating Appliances, a medium-sized company undergoing a period of expansion, were attracted to my proposals by the obvious, yet subtle, link and I was invited to meet and present my proposals in more detail.

The elusive ingredient which had been missing from my campaign for sponsorship finally appeared. Some people seem to be born with it, whilst the rest of us have to make it. Luck will thread its way through your motor racing both off and on the track.

Further lessons learnt

• Think laterally – your proposal needs to be unique and attractive to a sponsor, so out-of-the-ordinary ideas have a far better chance of success. Someone had the bright idea of getting a brewery to advertise a low-alcohol beer on their car – why wasn't it you or I?

• Address your mailshots to the relevant person if possible – there are always a number of management tiers and waste paper baskets between the postroom and the manager who holds the company's promotional budget.

• Tailor your proposal to make it relevant to your potential sponsor.

• Assistance need not necessarily be financial, and an advantage when it is not is that it avoids the need for the sponsor to be overly concerned with value for money and the sponsored to feel like an employee. Examples of such assistance could include:

– A safe dry place to work on the car or store it between races.

– The loan of a towing vehicle or trailer.

– Access to free rolling road time, specialist tuning or advice.

• Keep your proposals realistic: your local wallpaper shop is not likely to back your assault on the British Touring Car Championship, but might just pay your entry fees for a local sprint or hillclimb series.

• Never give up.

First impressions are important, and for my initial meeting I took along some colour photographs of the car and details of my previous results and had already worked out how much money was needed and in what areas. I had these typed out on a single sheet of A4 paper, which effectively acted as an agenda for our discussions and gave the right impression of being businesslike.

This advanced preparation also had the added effect of

forcing me to think through my basic proposals in more detail and provide a clear definition of what I could offer and expected in return. This meant that I was largely prepared for the majority of questions and could respond with more confidence.

Eventually, after some clarification of detail, my proposals were accepted in principle and I left agreeing to write and confirm the various points of our discussion in the form of a contract. This is reproduced below and takes the form of a sponsorship agreement containing the expectations of both parties as well as the more tangible issues.

SPONSORSHIP AGREEMENT

This agreement has been drawn up to consolidate ideas and to provide a clear direction by outlining the various responsibilities, expectations and actions of both parties, namely ....(Driver) and ....Managing Director (Sponsor).

THE ACTIVITY

Competing in 11 rounds of the *MG Enthusiast Magazine* Cup in a 'Class B' MG Metro. At this stage, exact dates and venues are still to be finally confirmed but provisional dates are as follows:

6TH MARCH	CADWELL PARK	MGCC
2ND APRIL	SNETTERTON	JAGUAR CC
24TH APRIL	DONINGTON PARK	
21ST MAY	SILVERSTONE	MGCC
2ND JULY	PEMBREY	JAGUAR CC
3RD SEPT	CADWELL PARK	JAGUAR CC
24TH SEPT	SNETTERTON	MGCC
TBA	SILVERSTONE	
TBA	CASTLE COMBE	

TBA   MALLORY PARK
TBA   THRUXTON

An agreed set of dates and venues will be available in early January.

EXPECTATIONS OF SPONSOR

a) The promotion of the 'Harton Metro' name and products by the Driver through participation and as set out in the section on Promotional Activities below.

b) A professional and responsible attitude by the driver at all times.

c) Confidentiality of Company information.

d) Close liaison and a 'team approach' throughout the season.

EXPECTATIONS OF DRIVER

a) Financial assistance to the sum of £.... as set out below.

b) Support and assistance as discussed in the form of the use of the sponsor's premises for storing the vehicle and trailer.

c) The ability to undertake maintenance and repairs at the sponsor's premises by prior arrangement.

d) The nomination of a specific Harton employee to act as a first point of contact and assist in administrative duties such as: sending out mailshots to business contacts; assisting with press releases; co-ordinating the sponsor's race day arrangements.

PROMOTIONAL ACTIVITIES

a) Sponsor's name, logos etc. displayed prominently on the car (N.B. any additional decals to the car are to be agreed by the sponsor in advance but already include those of the engine builder, car manufacturer and championship sponsor). Livery design is to be specified by the sponsor.

b) Attendance for photographic 'shoots' of the car and the sponsor's products if required.

c) Selected use of the car plus driver at promotional events organized by the sponsor by mutual agreement.

d) The production of regular press releases to trade press, selected articles and accompanying promotion in racing publications.

e) Attendance by the sponsor and his invited guests to race meetings – additional tickets to be arranged by the Harton representative.

f) The production of a small number of ancillary promotional items such as badges, car stickers featuring an association of car and products, subject to a separate proposal and costing exercise prepared for the sponsor's consideration.

FINANCIAL DETAILS

The Sponsor will pay the Driver £.... nett of income tax in the form of three equal payments at the beginning of December, February and March. Further payments are only anticipated by both parties if the vehicle is subject to extreme race damage and would be a matter of separate negotiation.

INSURANCES

The driver agrees to arrange personal accident insurance whilst racing and absolves the Sponsor of any liabilities or obligations arising out of any racing activity by the driver.

Whilst this may all seem rather formal, it was useful in many ways in adding a structure to what otherwise could have been a very *ad hoc* arrangement and it helped to define what we both hoped to achieve. In any sponsorship arrangement there are different viewpoints and goals that can easily be forgotten, misunderstood or conflict unless they are declared upfront. A failure to do so could mean a difference of opinion later, with disastrous results.

It is important to be realistic in setting out your obligations in the agreement as a sponsor will take a very dim view of you trying to ask for more money or time later on. For this reason I tried to assess thoroughly the estimated costs and achievable timespans for car preparation and so forth, before commitment.

In our case, once we were both happy with the agreement, I set out a proper detailed programme of when I intended to have the car available for photographs, and suggested various ideas, concluding with the most obvious option of surrounding the car with its namesake products. I also enclosed a draft sketch of suggested colour schemes and layouts for their company name, logos and so on. Understandably, these changed slightly in size and position following practical advice from a sign-making company, but generally the ideas in the original sketch can be seen on the finished item.

Publicity

If you have reached the heady heights of having a sponsor, an agreement, and even possibly a cheque, it would be easy to relax at this stage and think of how you should best spend it. Instead, you should concentrate your mind on the practicalities of delivering your part of the bargain, which is generally to raise the profile of your sponsor through your activities. To do this successfully you will benefit considerably by having a marketing plan.

Do not let the thought of this overwhelm you – the best marketing plans are very simple and seek to define how you are going to present paint, cornflakes or, in your case, your sponsor's name or products in the best way possible. Typically, you should concentrate on three main areas: the car, promotional material and the media.

Car livery

To begin with, it is likely that your sponsor already has a corporate image and a house style, even if it is just a colour theme to their delivery vans or standardized lettering to their letterhead and other stationary, perhaps incorporating a logo. It is essential that you obtain agreed examples of these to ensure that you follow them exactly: some companies have very strict control over their image to the extent that precise colour shades and text type must be used, and these will have to be incorporated exactly into your proposals.

The actual car is probably the biggest statement being made, so make sure it is eye-catching and shows off your sponsor's name to the full. If your sponsor identifies with particular colours, these should also be reflected in the livery of the car. Remember, when preparing sketches and ideas, to allow for the competition numbers that need to be displayed on the front bonnet and both sides of the car, together with any additional championship sponsor's decals that may have to be carried – these are usually defined in the race series regulations.

Even if you are particularly artistic, it is worth consulting a sign-making company early in the design process once you have a rough idea of what you are trying to achieve, as their advice will be invaluable. Large areas of colour are best spray-painted onto the car whilst lettering and logos are best applied as vinyl stickers. Advances in computer-controlled cutting has meant that virtually any design can be produced in any colour, subject to size and cost. Early advice will therefore help you considerably – for example, a monolithic panel of your sponsor's name may look good on paper, but if part of it becomes race-damaged you will have to replace all of it. A better method is to have each vinyl letter cut separately. Also, for the same reason, try to keep lettering high on the bodywork and consistent with body panel sizes.

Once you have a few livery options, make sure that the sponsor is consulted and involved in selecting the final design and agrees to the cost if this is not contained within your agreement.

Promotional material

It is fairly easy to develop a theme through the car's livery into other promotional items which are ancillary to your racing and the sponsor's name or product. The whole area of promotional material is quite wide, so it should be defined in your agreement or discussed at an early stage so that matters of cost, numbers and overall designs can be agreed in advance.

Examples of successful areas of promotional material include car stickers, leaflets, badges, T-shirts – the list is seemingly endless – but in all cases, in order to be successful they must give a clear message and hit the right audience. For this reason it is best to try to target your sponsor's main business contacts, a matter that needs to be planned in advance, well before the start of the season. Even a letterhead can start to make you seem like a 'proper' race team and give you an identity to be developed further in the future.

The media

One of the key benefits that you will have emphasized in your sponsorship proposals is the publicity that you will be able to attract for the company through the media. But do not think that the car itself will to guarantee sufficient interest alone because at the race circuits it will simply be one of many. Instead, consider the variety of opportunities – press, even radio and television – open to you to let people know what you are doing. Again, a planned approach will make this process easier and you should consider the following areas:

Press releases

These should be typed in double-line spacing with the text able to be accommodated on a single A4 page. They should be concise, providing details of what you are trying to communicate in the least number of words and with minimum verbiage – let the journalists embellish. Quotes from the sponsor, or even yourself, should be included to make them more lively, but again these should be brief. Each press release should be accompanied by a suitable photograph and any relevant promotional material that you have available.

Photographs should be in black and white and captioned on the reverse, giving your name, address and telephone number with a brief description. You may know that it is the Managing Director handing over a cheque, but the recipient will not unless told. As regards newsworthiness, the times of maximum impact include:

- The launch of the sponsorship deal itself.
- When the car is prepared and resplendent in its new livery outside the sponsor's business premises.
- When you are successful on the track!

Consider sending press releases to the following:

- Local newspapers.
- Trade magazines.
- Specialist publications.

Apart from the initial launch, press releases should be prepared and sent out at milestones in the season, such as immediately after a class or outright win, or at the half-way stage of your race programme. You may also wish to approach local newspapers to see if they would like to promote and cover any 'home' events that should appeal to local readers.

Radio

Local radio stations are always in need of interesting programmes and news, so they should not be discounted from your plans. In the first instance you should send them a press release, but why not accompany it with a letter asking them if they would consider following your progress throughout the season? This would provide the radio station with a useful source of material and guarantee your sponsor regular coverage. Even an interview on local radio is a start.

Television

With the advent of satellite television the need for new broadcasting material is increasing, although some will say that the quality of the coverage has suffered because the need for cheaper programmes has been reflected in the standard of their production. On a positive note, however, the increased air time available means that you have a better chance of achieving coverage. The advice offered under the 'Radio' section above is equally valid here, but your chances of success are likely to be limited unless your sponsorship link is unique. Television coverage is more likely to be obtained through coverage of the event itself, which can be a major factor when you are deciding which series to enter.

How to retain your sponsor

Imagine it is mid-season, you have had a few good results and are currently lying second in the championship. At your next race meeting it is wet and you are driving on the edge of your abilities and the car's traction. Ahead, a backmarker spins and your inside front wheel touches the grass and digs in. You correct it, but it is too late; in an instant you're going backwards, the other cars are streaming past and you apply full lock, full brakes, but the car keeps sliding and bumping over the wet grass until it meets the Armco barrier.

You emerge unscathed, but you have dented your pride and, unfortunately, the full length of the car, and the resulting damage is way beyond the capability of your immediate finances to repair.

If, on the Monday morning, you telephone your sponsor and are met by the words "Who are you?", you can probably surmise that your chances of further financial assistance will be slim.

Now, imagine the same situation, except that you had kept your sponsor up to date with your progress and as a result they realized where you were placed in the championship. Knowing the importance of yesterday's race, it is even possible that they were at the track to watch your valiant efforts and, therefore, your 'incident'. Even if they had been unable to attend, they might still have contemplated over Sunday lunch that it was a lousy day outside. This should at least guarantee some sympathy for your plight and perhaps lead to a positive response to any request you need to make for further assistance.

Like marriage, the most important point to remember about sponsorship is that it is a two-way partnership which depends on effective and timely communication between both parties. To add further comparisons, understanding and commitment is needed from both sides or an inevitable breakdown of the relationship will surely follow.

Earlier in this book I tried to stress the importance of presentation and the positive contribution it can make to your racing, whether at amateur or professional level. Similar care will be needed when dealing with a sponsor in order to secure a good working relationship and to be able to extend it to following seasons and possibly other ventures. These may include another rung up the ladder of success to a better car or a more prestigious race series and, therefore, almost certainly will be more costly.

Communication can be as simple as the occasional chat on

the telephone, but it is more likely to be noted and remembered if you present any information in a proper format such as a newsletter. Also, by making it easy to digest, this can be sent to the sponsor's main contacts, thereby achieving wider circulation, which can only be beneficial to both of you.

I am not suggesting that you embark on a self-publicity campaign – although I doubt if any of us know many shrinking violets in the racing fraternity – but rather that you present information clearly and professionally. If this is not your forte, why not speak to your friends, who may be able to act on your behalf? The information could perhaps take the form of a bulletin or newssheet – it all depends on the circumstances.

Examples of items to report include:

• Details of your agreed championship venues and dates plus an invitation to any test days you may have arranged.

• Any coverage of the car in the press.

• Good quality photographs of the car in action on the track.

• Achievements such as being placed in class, breaking any lap records and your position in the race series.

• Disasters that may have an effect on your agreement, for example if you blow up an engine this week it may not be possible to race next week. Honesty is always the best policy.

As already mentioned, the sponsor will expect you, your car and, more importantly, your attitude to reflect the product or company image in a positive manner. This expectation, even if not forming part of the formal agreement, is one that must always be borne in mind and fulfilled: being courteous, articulate and accessible may not be part of your normal demeanour, but it will need to become so if you expect to progress.

This continuing emphasis on image is deliberate because in the end it will determine whether or not a sponsor feels relaxed about your activities and is assured that they are reflecting well on the company. If you are not projecting the required image effectively, your sponsor may well start to question whether they are getting value for money, and remember that in extreme circumstances you could even be damaging their reputation.

This does not necessarily mean that you must win, or even finish, every race, but rather that the interests of your sponsor must always be uppermost in your mind – this, to some, is the price that needs to be paid.

Simple care and attention, such as sending your sponsor a map of how to get to the next race meeting, will be appreciated. It is also a good idea to enclose details of the facilities available, an outline of the day's events, guidance on some of the best places to view the action, and anything else that may be useful, especially if your sponsor has not been to any of the circuits before. Anyway, it does no harm to be helpful.

If you can manage a press release, an end-of-season report is also not that difficult to put together. This should consist of photos, race reports, lap times and, most importantly, any news clippings, accompanied by a covering letter to thank your sponsors for all their assistance during the season. This is also the ideal time to start discussing both of your aims for the year ahead. Good luck!

APPENDIX

Useful addresses

The following is a selection from the many hundreds of companies and associations active in the UK in the field of motorsport. Their inclusion in this listing should not be construed as any endorsement either by the author or by the publisher.

**ACCESSORIES AND COMPONENTS
INCLUDING PERFORMANCE EQUIPMENT**

AUTOSPRINT
29 Gough Street, Holloway Head, Birmingham B1 1HN
Tel: 0121 236 5133
Fax: 0121 631 2876

AVONBAR RACING
219 New Haw Road, Addlestone, Weybridge, Surrey KT15 2DP
Tel: 01932 842024
Fax: 01932 858317

BURTON PERFORMANCE CENTRE
631 Eastern Avenue, Ilford, Essex IG2 6PN
Tel: 0181 554 2281
Fax: 0181 554 4828

BLYDENSTEIN ENGINEERING LTD
Hyde Hall Farm, Sandon, Buntingford,
Hertfordshire SG9 0RU
Tel: 01763 272866

BM MOTORSPORT LTD
Unit 33, Silverstone Circuit, Silverstone, Towcester,
Northamptonshire NN12 8TN
Tel: 01327 857875
Fax: 01327 857653

CROYDON RACE & RALLY CENTRE
279/283 Portland Road, South Norwood,
London SE25 4QQ
Tel: 0181 656 7031
Fax: 0181 654 9723

DATUM CARBURETTOR SERVICES
180 Hersham Road, Hersham, Walton on Thames,
Surrey KT12 5QE
Tel: 01932 221955 & 232525
Fax: 01932 232525

DEMON TWEEKS
Hugmore Lane, Llan-y-Pwll, Wrexham, Clwyd LL13 9YE
Tel: 01978 664466
Fax: 01978 664467

EARS MOTORSPORT & 4X4 CENTRE
The Wharf, Buxton Road, Macclesfield,
Cheshire SK10 1LZ
Tel: 01625 433773
Fax: 01625 433614

ELITE
136/138 New Road, Rainham, Essex RM13 8DE
Tel: 01708 525577
Fax: 01708 556684

EUROPA SPECIALIST SPARES
Fauld Industrial Park, Tutbury, Burton upon Trent, Staffordshire
DE13 9HR
Tel: 01283 815609
Fax: 01283 814976

GRAND PRIX RACEWEAR
10 The Broadway, Gunnersbury Lane, London W3 8HR
Tel: 0181 993 7555
Fax: 0181 993 5502

HOOPERS MOTORSPORT PARTS
1 Maypole Square, Church Road, Hanham,
Bristol BS15 3AA
Tel: 01179 676563 & 674732
Fax: 01179 352901

KENT PERFORMANCE CAMSHAFTS LTD
Units 1-4 Military Road, Shorncliffe Industrial Estate, Folkestone,
Kent CT20 3SP
Tel: 01303 248666
Fax: 01303 252508

LARKSPEED PERFORMANCE CENTRE
34 Bradford Road, Cleckheaton, Yorkshire BD19 3LN
Tel: 01274 877787
Fax: 01274 873853
249/251 Anlaby Road, Hull, Humberside HU3 2SE
Tel: 01482 581035
Fax: 01482 581002
Arndale Centre, Crossgates, Leeds, Yorkshire LS15 8NW
Tel: 01132 643231
Fax: 01132 602495

95 Sheffield Road, Rotherham, South Yorkshire S60 1DA
Tel: 01709 361105
Fax: 01709 830308

MAGNEX PERFORMANCE EXHAUSTS
Birchwood Way, Cotes Park Industrial Estate, Somercotes,
Derbyshire DE55 4QQ
Tel: 01773 831999
Fax: 01773 830922

PIPER RS LTD
2 St John's Court, Ashford Business Centre, Ashford,
Kent TN24 0SJ
Tel: 01233 500200
Fax: 01233 500300

PIPERCROSS
Filtration House, Overstone Road, Moulton,
Northampton NN3 1UL
Tel: 01604 671100
Fax: 01604 671101

PRODRIVE LTD
Acorn Way, Banbury, Oxon OX16 7XS
Tel: 01295 273355
Fax: 01295 271188

PRO-SPORT
14 Granville Road, Melton Mowbray,
Leicestershire LE13 0SN
Tel: 01664 501982
Fax: 01664 501762

RE PERFORMANCE CENTRE
Bridge Street, Freetown, Bury, Lancashire BL9 6HH
Tel: 0161 761 1177
Fax: 0161 761 5194

RIPSPEED RACING LTD
54 Fore Street, Edmonton, London N18 2SS
Tel: 0181 803 4344
Fax: 0181 345 5750

ROAD & RACING ACCESSORIES LTD
75-77 Moore Park Road, Fulham, London SW6 2HH
Tel: 0171 736 2881
Fax: 0171 736 6116

ROAD & STAGE MOTORSPORT
Whitegate, White Lund Trading Estate, Morecambe, Lancashire
LA3 3BS
Tel: 01524 844066
Fax: 01524 841813

ROADRUNNER
379 Nuthall Road, Aspley, Nottingham NG8 5BU
Tel: 0115 978 1173
Fax: 0115 942 3054

SMART CAR
59 Station Road, Beeston, Nottingham NG9 2AP
Tel: 0115 922 9944
Fax: 0115 943 1496

SPARCO UK
52 Tanners Drive, Blakelands, Milton Keynes, Buckinghamshire
MK14 5BW
Tel: 01908 216916
Fax: 01908 217726

STOCKBRIDGE RACING LTD
High Street, Stockbridge, Hampshire SO20 6HE
Tel: 0264 810712
Fax: 0264 810247

SUPERCHIPS LTD
2-10 Homestall, Buckingham Industrial Park,
Buckingham MK18 1XJ
Tel: 01280 816781
Fax: 01280 816764

TAR.OX
98 White Hart Lane, Wood Green, London N22 5SG
Tel: 0181 888 2354
Fax: 0181 881 0497
Unit 1, Rutland Street, Bradford, Yorkshire BD4 7EA
Tel: 01274 733 727
Fax: 01274 723 890

CLUBS

RAC MOTOR SPORTS ASSOCIATION LTD
Motor Sports House, Riverside Park, Colnbrook, Slough,
Berkshire SL3 0HG
Tel: 01753 681736
Fax: 01753 682938

(A full listing of recognized motorsport-organizing clubs together
with the competition calendar for the current season is available
from the RACMSA.)

BRITISH AUTOMOBILE RACING CLUB LTD
Thruxton Circuit, Thruxton, Andover, Hants SP11 8PN
Tel: 01264 772607
Fax: 01264 773794

BARC (PEMBREY) LTD
Pembrey Circuit, Llanelli, Dyfed SP11 8PN
Tel: 01554 891042
Fax: 01554 891347

BRITISH NATIONAL DRAG RACING ASSOCIATION
General Secretary: Mrs Anne Pallant, 105 Parkfield Crescent,
Ruislip, Middlesex HA4 0RD
Tel: 0181 864 6232

BRITISH STOCK CAR ASSOCIATION
Long Eaton Stadium, Long Eaton,
Nottinghamshire NG10 2DU.
Secretary: Mrs M Welling, 5 Darley Road, Edmonton, London N9
Tel: 0181 360 7978

BRITISH RACING DRIVERS' CLUB LTD
Silverstone Circuit, Silverstone, Towcester,
Northants NN12 8TN
Tel: 01327 857271
Fax: 01327 857296

CIRCUITS AND DRIVING SCHOOLS

BRANDS HATCH RACING CENTRE
Brands Hatch Circuit, Fawkham, Dartford, Kent DA3 8NG
Tel: 01474 872367
Fax: 01474 874766

CADWELL PARK RACING CIRCUIT
The Old Manor House, Cadwell Park, Louth,
Lincolnshire LN11 9SE
Tel: 01507 343248
Fax: 01507 343519

CASTLE COMBE RACING SCHOOL
Castle Combe Circuit, Chippenham, Wiltshire SN14 7EY
Tel: 01249 782417
Fax: 01249 782392

EVERYMAN MOTOR RACING DRIVERS' SCHOOL
Mallory Park Circuit, Kirkby Mallory, Leicestershire LE9 7QE
Tel: 01455 841670
Fax: 01455 848289

JIM RUSSELL RACING DRIVERS SCHOOL
Donington Park Circuit, Castle Donington, Derbyshire DE74 2RP
Tel: 01332 811430
Fax: 01332 811422

KNOCKHILL RACING AND RALLY SCHOOL
Knockhill Racing Circuit, Dunfermline, Fife KY12 9TF
Tel: 01383 723337
Fax: 01383 620167

OULTON PARK RACING CENTRE
Oulton Park Circuit, Little Budworth, Tarporley,
Cheshire CW6 9BW
Tel: 01829 760381 & 760301
Fax: 01829 760378

SILVERSTONE JOHN WATSON PERFORMANCE DRIVING
CENTRE
Silverstone Circuit, Silverstone, Towcester,
Northamptonshire NN12 8TN
Tel: 01327 857177
Fax: 01327 858268

SNETTERTON RACING CENTRE
Snetterton Circuit, Norwich, Norfolk NR16 2JU
Tel: 01953 887303
Fax: 01953 888220

THRUXTON CIRCUIT
Andover, Hants SP11 8PN
Tel: 01264 772607 & 772696
Fax: 01264 773794